Prentice Hall

LITERATURE
Timeless Voices, Timeless Themes

Literary Analysis
for Enrichment

THE AMERICAN EXPERIENCE

Prentice
Hall

Upper Saddle River, New Jersey
Glenview, Illinois
Needham, Massachusetts

ISBN 0-13-062864-6

5 6 7 8 9 10   05

CONTENTS

UNIT 4: DIVISION, RECONCILIATION, AND EXPANSION (1850–1914)

UNIT 5: DISILLUSION, DEFIANCE, AND DISCONTENT (1914–1946)

UNIT 6: PROSPERITY AND PROTEST (1946–PRESENT)

Name _____ Date _____

"The Earth on Turtle's Back" (Onondaga)
"When Grizzlies Walked Upright" (Modoc)
from *The Navajo Origin Legend* (Navaho)
from *The Iroquois Constitution* (Iroquois)

Literary Analysis: Comparing Origin Myths

Origin myths are traditional stories that recount the beginnings of life on Earth. These myths often explain such phenomena as the beginning of human life, the customs and beliefs of a people, the creation of features of the landscape, and events beyond people's control. Origin myths involve gods, spirits, animals, and the elements in their explanations.

DIRECTIONS: On the lines provided, compare the three creation myths (Onondaga, Modoc, and Navajo) by briefly explaining the role of animals, elements, or spirits and gods in each one.

1. **The role of animals**

_____

_____

_____

_____

_____

_____

_____

_____

2. **The role of the elements (earth, wind, fire, water)**

_____

_____

_____

_____

_____

_____

_____

_____

3. **The role of spirits or gods**

_____

_____

_____

_____

_____

_____

_____

_____

"A Journey Through Texas" from *The Journey of Alvar Núñez Cabeza de Vaca*
by Alvar Núñez Cabeza de Vaca
"Boulders Taller Than the Great Tower of Seville"
by García López de Cárdenas

Literary Analysis: Comparing and Contrasting Narratives

"A Journey Through Texas" and "Boulders Taller Than the Great Tower of Seville" are both **exploration narratives**—firsthand accounts of people's journeys into new lands. Exploration narratives generally focus on the difficulties that the explorers faced and the specific discoveries they made. Explorers wrote both to inform readers about other lands and to express their own personal reactions to the people, places, and things they saw there. Writers of exploration narratives may also try to impress readers with tales of their courage, or inspire them to go exploring on their own.

DIRECTIONS: Compare and contrast these two exploration narratives by filling in the following chart. For the categories listed, give examples of similarities and differences. Then answer the question that follows.

Category	Similarities	Differences
1. **treatment of Native Americans**		
2. **reaction to American landscape**		
3. **hardships faced**		

4. Which exploration narrative seems more personal? Which one seems more aimed at impressing others? Explain your opinions.

_____

_____

_____

_____

_____

Name _____ Date _____

from *The Interesting Narrative of the Life of Olaudah Equiano*
by Olaudah Equiano

Literary Analysis: Slave and Exploration Narratives

A **slave narrative** is an autobiographical account of life as a slave. It documents a slave's experiences from his or her point of view. The selection from Equiano's narrative provides an especially grim description of the long voyage from Africa to Barbados that he was forced to endure when he was only eleven years old.

Slave narratives share many elements with other types of personal narratives. They express personal viewpoints and reactions, while at the same time providing factual information.

DIRECTIONS: Think back to the two **exploration narratives** you read. Then compare and contrast Equiano's **slave narrative** with those narratives by answering the questions that follow.

1. What is one similarity between Equiano's journey and the journeys of the explorers? What is one difference?

   _____

   _____

   _____

   _____

2. How do the slavers treat Equiano? How do the Native Americans treat the explorers?

   _____

   _____

   _____

   _____

3. Do you see any similarity between the slavers' treatment of Equiano and the explorers' treatment of the Native Americans? Explain.

   _____

   _____

   _____

   _____

4. What do you think is the most important difference between Equiano's narrative and those of the explorers?

   _____

   _____

   _____

   _____

Name _____   Date _____

from *Journal of the First Voyage to America* by Christopher Columbus

Literary Analysis: Journals and Tone

When keeping a **journal**, a writer may be motivated to shade the events he or she describes in a favorable or unfavorable way. Christopher Columbus's journals, for example, were meant to be read by the Spanish monarchs responsible for funding his expeditions. As you read a journal like Columbus's, pay attention to the writer's **tone**—the attitude that he or she conveys. Tone can indicate a writer's bias, or ulterior purpose. To identify tone, look for the writer's choice of details and use of descriptive words.

DIRECTIONS: Read the following excerpts from Columbus's *Journal of the First Voyage to America* and answer the questions that follow.

> Sunday, Oct. 21st [1492]. At 10 o'clock, we arrived at the cape of the island, and anchored, the other vessels in company. After having dispatched a meal, I went ashore, and found no habitation save a single house, and that without an occupant; we had no doubt that the people had fled in terror at our approach, as the house was completely furnished. I suffered nothing to be touched, and went with my captains and some of the crew to view the country.

1. What does this passage indicate about Columbus's relationship with both the inhabitants of the island and his crew?

    _____
    _____
    _____

2. Describe the tone of the passage. What details and word choices contribute to this tone?

    _____
    _____
    _____

3. What message might Columbus have hoped to convey to his audience through this tone?

    _____
    _____

> This island even exceeds the others in beauty and fertility. Groves of lofty and flourishing trees are abundant, as also large lakes, surrounded and overhung by the foliage, in a most enchanting manner. Everything looked as green as in April in Andalusia. The melody of the birds was so exquisite that one was never willing to part from the spot, and the flocks of parrots obscured the heavens.

4. Describe the tone of this passage. What details and word choices contribute to this tone?

    _____
    _____

5. What message might Columbus have hoped to convey to his audience through the use of this tone?

    _____
    _____

Name _____ Date _____

from *The General History of Virginia* by John Smith
from *Of Plymouth Plantation* by William Bradford

Literary Analysis: Three Kinds of Historical Narratives

Historical narratives, like **exploration narratives** and **slave narratives,** are **narrative accounts,** or stories that describe real-life events. Some exploration narratives and slave narratives can also be considered historical narratives, since they deal with significant historical events. All share certain elements. They contain factual information, and, if they are firsthand accounts, may be subjective and/or contain inaccuracies.

DIRECTIONS: Compare these different narrative accounts by answering the questions.

> *The General History of Virginia*
> *Of Plymouth Plantation*
> "A Journey Through Texas"
> "Boulders Taller Than the Great Tower of Seville"
> *The Interesting Narrative of the Life of Olaudah Equiano*

1. Where does each of these accounts take place?

_____
_____
_____
_____
_____

2. What are the subjects of each of these narrative accounts?

_____
_____
_____
_____
_____

3. Do you consider all of these accounts historical narratives? In other words, do you feel that they all contain significant historical events? Explain your opinion.

_____
_____
_____
_____
_____

4. Which one of these accounts did you enjoy reading most? Why?

_____
_____
_____
_____
_____

"To My Dear and Loving Husband" by Anne Bradstreet
"Huswifery" by Edward Taylor

Literary Analysis: Analyzing a Conceit and Comparing Themes

"Huswifery" features an excellent example of a **conceit,** an elaborate and unusual comparison between two startlingly different subjects. Conceits are often lengthy and intricate, frequently developing through a series of shorter, less elaborate comparisons into the framework for an entire poem. Like the seventeenth-century English poets John Donne and George Herbert, whose work he greatly admired, Edward Taylor often used extended conceits in his writing. Yet, while Donne and Herbert used conceits primarily to surprise or shock readers, Taylor used conceits to emphasize the close relationship between God and the natural world.

1. "Huswifery" is framed around a conceit comparing the making of cloth with the granting of God's grace. What do each of the following lines from the poem suggest?

   a. "And make my soul Thy holy spoole to be."

   _____

   _____

   b. "That I am clothed in holy robes for glory."

   _____

   _____

2. Taylor believed that the granting of grace involved the transformation of a person from a flawed and imperfect state of being into a state of purity and perfection. How does Taylor's conceit express this belief?

   _____

   _____

A **theme** is a central message or insight about life revealed by a literary work. Sometimes, poets reveal their themes directly. More often, themes are revealed indirectly through the writer's use of figurative language—language that is not meant to be interpreted literally. For this reason, it is essential to look beyond the literal meaning of the words in a poem and try to determine their underlying meaning.

3. What is the theme of "To My Dear and Loving Husband"? Is the theme reveal directly or indirectly? Support your answer.

   _____

   _____

4. What is the theme of "Huswifery"? How is the theme conveyed?

   _____

   _____

5. Compare the themes of the two poems. What common threads can you find? How are the common threads connected to the Puritan beliefs of the poets? Why would it be unlikely for Taylor to have ever written a poem like "To My Dear and Loving Husband"?

   _____

   _____

Name _____ Date _____

from *Sinners in the Hands of an Angry God* by Jonathan Edwards

Literary Analysis: Sermon as Persuasive Appeal

A **sermon** is a speech given from a pulpit in a house of worship, usually as part of a religious service. Jonathan Edwards was known for his "fire-and-brimstone" sermons, which carried warnings about the torments of hell. These sermons were a type of **persuasive appeal;** they were intended to persuade the listeners by appealing to their emotions.

DIRECTIONS: Read the excerpts from Edwards's sermon. Then answer the questions.

How dreadful is the state of those that are daily and hourly in the danger of this great wrath and infinite misery! But this is the dismal case of every soul in this congregation that has not been born again, however moral and strict, sober and religious, they may otherwise be. Oh, that you would consider it, whether you be young or old! … Those of you that finally continue in a natural condition, that shall keep you out of Hell longest will be there in a little time! Your damnation does not slumber; it will come swiftly, and, in all probability, very suddenly…

1. What feeling is Edwards trying to arouse in the listener? Explain.

   _____

   _____

Many are daily coming from the east, west, north and south; many that were very lately in the same miserable condition that you are in, are now in a happy state, with their hearts filled with love to him who has loved them, and washed them from their sins in his own blood, and rejoicing in hope of the glory of God. How awful it is to be left behind at such a day! To see so many others feasting, while you are pining and perishing!

2. What does Edwards offer to those who accept his message? What will become of those who don't?

   _____

   _____

   _____

O sinner! Consider the fearful danger you are in: it is a great furnace of wrath, a wide and bottomless pit, full of the fire of wrath, that you are held over in the hand of that God, whose wrath is provoked and incensed as much against you, as against many of the damned in Hell. You hang by a slender thread, with the flames of divine wrath flashing about it, and ready every moment to singe it, and burn it asunder; and you have no interest in any mediator, and nothing to lay hold of to save yourself, nothing to keep off the flames of wrath, nothing of your own, nothing that you have ever done, nothing that you can do, to induce God to spare you one moment.…

3. How does Edwards use repetition in describing God and sinners? To which emotions is this repetition meant to appeal?

   _____

   _____

   _____

   _____

   _____

   _____

from *The Autobiography* and **from *Poor Richard's Almanack*** by Benjamin Franklin

Literary Analysis: Fact and Opinion

In personal writing, events or information are often viewed from the perspective of the person who wrote or experienced them. At the same time, they can be less objective. For this reason, it is important to be able to **distinguish fact from opinion** when reading personal writings. Opinions state personal beliefs or preferences and cannot be proved. Facts, on the other hand, can be proved.

DIRECTIONS: Read these excerpts from Franklin's *Autobiography* and *Poor Richard's Almanack*. On the lines provided, write whether each statement represents fact or opinion.

_____ 1. It was about this time I conceived the bold and arduous project of arriving at moral perfection. I wished to live without committing any fault at any time…

_____ 2 …the mere speculative conviction that it was our interest to be completely virtuous was not sufficient to prevent our slipping; and that the contrary habits must be broken, and good ones acquired and established, before we can have any dependence on a steady, uniform rectitude of conduct.

_____ 3. In the various enumerations of the moral virtues I had met with in my reading, I found the catalog more or less numerous, as different writers included more or fewer ideas under the same name. Temperance, for example, was by some confined to eating and drinking, while by others it was extended to mean the moderating every other pleasure, appetite, inclination, or passion, bodily or mental, even to our avarice and ambition.

_____ 4. …I included under thirteen names of virtues all that at that time occurred to me as necessary or desirable…

_____ 5. I made a little book, in which I allotted a page for each of the virtues. I ruled each page with red ink, so as to have seven columns, one for each day of the week, marking each column with a letter for the day.

_____ 6. But, on the whole, though I never arrived at the perfection I had been so ambitious of obtaining, but fell far short of it, yet I was, by the endeavor, a better and a happier man than I otherwise would have been if I had not attempted it…

_____ 7. Fools make feasts, and wise men eat them.

_____ 8. A good example is the best sermon.

_____ 9. For want of a nail the shoe is lost; for want of a shoe the horse is lost; for want of a horse, the rider is lost.

Name _____ Date _____

"The Declaration of Independence" by Thomas Jefferson
from "The Crisis, Number 1" by Thomas Paine

Literary Analysis: Comparing and Contrasting Revolutionary Texts

1. The **tone** of a literary work is the author's attitude toward his or her subject. Compare the tone of the Declaration of Independence with that of Paine's essay. Cite passages from both texts to support your answer.

   _____

   _____

   _____

2. What is each writer's intended **audience**? How does the audience affect the way in which each piece is written? Support your answer.

   _____

   _____

3. Compare the two authors' **purposes**. What similarities can you identify between the two writers' purposes? Which writer do you feel is more successful in achieving his purpose? Support your answer.

   _____

   _____

   _____

4. **Parallelism** is the repeated use of phrases, clauses, or sentences that are similar in structure or meaning. Writers use this technique to emphasize important ideas, create rhythm, and make their writing forceful and direct. In the Declaration of Independence, Jefferson uses parallelism when listing the reasons that Americans felt compelled to declare their independence. Explain how Jefferson's use of parallelism makes his argument grow stronger with each reason he presents. Then tell how his use of parallelism helps to make his writing memorable.

   _____

   _____

   _____

5. An **aphorism** is a short, pointed statement expressing a wise or clear observation or a general truth. Thomas Paine uses aphorisms throughout his essay to make his argument strong and memorable. By defending the American cause through a series of statements expressing general truths, how does Paine create the impression that the American forces are fighting not only for their own independence but also for the cause of liberty and justice for all humankind?

   _____

   _____

6. In what way are the **themes**, or central messages, of the two pieces similar? How do the themes differ?

   _____

   _____

Name _____ Date _____

"To His Excellency, General Washington" and **"An Hymn to the Evening"**
by Phillis Wheatley

Literary Analysis: Comparing the Use of Personification

Personification is a type of figurative language which gives human powers and characteristics to something that is not human, such as an object, an aspect of nature, or an abstract idea. For example, in the line "Anon Britannia droops the pensive head," Britannia (England) is compared to a person who bows her head in thought.

DIRECTIONS: Read these stanzas from "An Hymn to the Evening" and answer the questions that follow.

> Soon as the sun forsook the eastern main
> The pealing thunder shook the heav'nly plain;
> Majestic grandeur! From the zephyr's wing,
> Exhales the incense of the blooming spring.
> Soft purl the streams, the birds renew their notes,
> And through the air their mingled music floats.
>
> Through all the heav'ns what beauteous dyes are spread!
> But the west glories in the deepest red:
> So may our breasts with ev'ry virtue glow,
> The living temples of our God below!

1. Identify each example of personification contained in these stanzas. Which human characteristics are being given to nonhuman objects?

_____

_____

_____

_____

2. In your opinion, what is the overall effect of the personification used in these lines?

_____

_____

_____

_____

3. Reread "To His Excellency, General Washington" and describe three examples of personification it contains.

_____

_____

_____

_____

_____

_____

"Speech in the Virginia Convention" by Patrick Henry
"Speech in the Convention" by Benjamin Franklin

Literary Analysis: Comparing Oratorical Techniques

Patrick Henry and Benjamin Franklin used some of the same oratorical techniques to emphasize important ideas. Their oratorical techniques include **repetition** of an idea in the same words; **restatement** of a key idea in different words; **parallelism,** or repeated use of grammatical structures; and **rhetorical questions,** or questions with obvious answers that are asked not because answers are expected but to stir the audience's emotions.

DIRECTIONS: Patrick Henry and Benjamin Franklin use the same techniques, but the effects of their speeches are quite different. In the following chart record one example of each oratorical technique from their speeches. If you can't find an example, write "None." Then answer the questions that follow.

Technique	Henry	Franklin
1. **Repetition**		
2. **Restatement**		
3. **Parallelism**		
4. **Rhetorical Questions**		

1. Which oratorical technique is not found in Franklin's speech? Why do you think Franklin may have avoided using this technique?

_____

_____

2. How does Henry's use of rhetorical questions differ from Franklin's?

_____

3. How would you describe the oratorical style of Patrick Henry?

_____

4. How would you describe Benjamin Franklin's oratorical style?

_____

5. Which speech, in your opinion, is more effective? Explain.

_____

_____

_____

"Letter to Her Daughter from the New White House" by Abigail Adams
from *Letters from an American Farmer* by Michel-Guillaume Jean de Crèvecoeur

Literary Analysis: Comparing Epistles

A **private letter**, such as the one Abigail Adams wrote to her daughter, is meant to be read only by the person to whom it is addressed. An **epistle,** on the other hand, is intended for the general public. Crèvecoeur wrote *Letters from an American Farmer* to inform the public about America. Martin Luther King, Jr., wrote his *Letter from Birmingham City Jail*, which you read earlier in this unit, to inspire readers to join the cause of civil rights.

DIRECTIONS: Compare the epistles of Crèvecoeur and King. Read the following passages. Then answer the questions on the lines provided.

> The American ought therefore to love this country much better than that wherein either he or his forebears were born. Here the rewards of his industry follow with equal steps the progress of his labor; his labor is founded on the basis of nature, *self-interest;* can it want a stronger allurement?
>
> —*Letters from an American Farmer*

> We will reach the goal of freedom in Birmingham and all over the nation, because the goal of America is freedom. Abused and scorned though we may be, our destiny is tied up with the destiny of America. Before the Pilgrims landed at Plymouth we were here. Before the pen of Jefferson etched across the pages of history the majestic words of the Declaration of Independence, we were here.
>
> —*Letter From Birmingham City Jail*

1. How is the style of these passages different from that of a personal letter?

   _____

   _____

2. List the oratorical technique that each writer uses in his epistle.

   _____

   _____

3. Why do you think Crèvecoeur and King use these oratorical techniques?

   _____

   _____

4. Why is the epistle an effective vehicle for Crèvecoeur's and King's ideas?

   _____

   _____

   _____

Name _____ Date _____

"The Devil and Tom Walker" by Washington Irving

Literary Analysis: Omniscient Narrator and Point of View

An **omniscient** (all-knowing) narrator is one who stands outside the action of a story and relates the thoughts and feelings of all the characters. The narrator shares these thoughts, ideas, and viewpoints with the reader, helping him or her to understand all the characters. The narrator may also comment on the characters and events.

DIRECTIONS: Read each passage and answer the questions on the lines provided.

> The lonely wayfarer shrunk within himself at the horrid clamor and clapperclawing; eyed the den of discord askance; and hurried on his way, rejoicing, if a bachelor, in his celibacy.

1. Whose point of view does the narrator reveal in this passage?

   _____

2. What do you learn about this character's feelings or beliefs?

   _____

> One day that Tom Walker had been to a distant part of the neighborhood, he took what he considered a shortcut homeward, through the swamp. Like most shortcuts, it was an ill-chosen route.

3. Whose point of view does the narrator reveal in this passage?

   _____

4. What do you learn about this character's feelings or beliefs?

   _____

> Tom recollected the tree which his black friend had just hewn down, and which was ready for burning. "Let the freebooter roast," said Tom, "who cares!" He now felt convinced that all he had heard and seen was no illusion.

5. Whose perspective does the narrator reveal in this passage?

   _____

6. What do you learn about this character's feelings or beliefs?

   _____

7. Suppose the story had been narrated by Tom Walker, instead of an omniscient narrator. Could all of these passages still be included in the story? Explain.

   _____

   _____

   _____

   _____

© Prentice-Hall, Inc.

Literary Analysis for Enrichment **13**

"A Psalm of Life" and **"The Tide Rises, The Tide Falls"**
by Henry Wadsworth Longfellow

Literary Analysis: Comparing Stanza Forms

Stanzas in poetry are units of two or more lines that share a common pattern of rhythm (or meter) and rhyme. Like a prose paragraph, each stanza usually develops a single main idea or explores a particular subject or image. Stanzas are named according to the number of lines they contain. For example, a two-line stanza is a **couplet;** a four-line stanza is a **quatrain;** and a five-line stanza is a **cinquain.**

DIRECTIONS: Compare and contrast the two stanzas by answering the questions on the lines provided.

A.

Life is real! Life is earnest!
    And the grave is not its goal;
Dust thou art, to dust returnest,
    Was not spoken of the soul.

—"A Psalm of Life"

B.

The morning breaks; the steeds in their stalls
Stamp and neigh, as the hostler calls:
The day returns, but nevermore
Returns the traveler to the shore.
    And the tide rises, the tide falls.

—"The Tide Rises, The Tide Falls"

1. What type of stanza does each poem use?

   A. _____   B. _____

2. Describe the end rhyme pattern in each stanza.

   A. _____   B. _____

3. What pattern of stressed syllables occurs in this stanza from "A Psalm of Life"? How does this pattern compare with the pattern of stressed syllables in this stanza from "The Tide Rises, The Tide Falls"?

   _____

   _____

   _____

   _____

   _____

   _____

4. How is the rhythmic pattern of each stanza appropriate to the overall message in the poem of which it is a part?

   _____

   _____

   _____

   _____

   _____

"Thanatopsis" by William Cullen Bryant
"Old Ironsides" by Oliver Wendell Holmes
"The First Snowfall" by James Russell Lowell
from *Snowbound* by John Greenleaf Whittier

Literary Analysis: Meter and Meaning

The **meter** of a poem is the rhythmic pattern created by stressed and unstressed syllables. The word *meter* comes from the Greek *metron,* which means "measure." The basic unit of meter is the foot, which contains a stressed syllable and one or more unstressed syllables.

The **iamb** is the most common type of foot in American and English verse. Both the type and the number of feet in the lines of a poem determine its meter. To find the meter of a poem, you must scan it, marking the stressed and unstressed syllables.

Iambic tetrameter (four iambs):	Unwarmed by any sunset light,
	The gray day darkened into night…
Iambic pentameter (five iambs):	And millions in those solitudes, since first
	The flight of years began, have laid them down
	In their last sleep—the dead reign there alone.

A poet's choice of meter affects the meaning of a poem. Iambic tetrameter, for example, is a simple, conversational meter. Iambic pentameter is more complex, allowing for longer lines and more development of abstract thought. Poets may also vary the meter of a line by altering the foot. This often affects the meaning of the poem. Metrical variation can indicate a quickening or slowing of action, or it can work to create a new moo

_____

_____

_____

_____

_____

_____

_____

_____

_____

_____

Name _____ Date _____

from **"Crossing the Great Divide"** by Meriwether Lewis
from **"The Most Sublime Spectacle on Earth"** by John Wesley Powell

Literary Analysis: Description and Descriptive Language

Description is writing that captures sights, sounds, smells, tastes, and physical sensations. Writers use two kinds of language when they describe.

Literal language gives an objective, factual description of a person, place, thing, or event.	I made McNeal cook the remainder of our meat which afforded a slight breakfast for ourselves and the Chief.
Figurative language describes imaginatively or poetically, using description that is not meant to be taken literally. The writer may use similes, metaphors, or personification, as in this example.	In this manner the little clouds seem to be individualized, to have wills and souls of their own, and to be going on diverse errands—a vast assemblage of self-willed clouds, faring here and there, intent upon purposes hidden in their own breasts.

DIRECTIONS: Read these passages from "Crossing the Great Divide" and "The Most Sublime Spectacle on Earth." Identify the descriptive language in each as literal or figurative and explain your identification.

1. Shortly after Capt. Clark arrived with the Interpreter Charbono, and the Indian woman, who proved to be a sister of the Chief Cameahwait.

   _____

   _____

2. When the clouds play in the canyon, as they often do in the rainy season, another set of effects is produced.

   _____

   _____

3. Great continental blocks are upheaved from beneath the sea by internal geologic forces that fashion the earth.

   _____

   _____

4. The adamant foundations of the earth have been wrought into a sublime harp, upon which the clouds of the heavens play with mighty tempests or with gentle showers.

   _____

   _____

5. At noon the canoes arrived, and we had the satisfaction once more to find ourselves all together, with a flattering prospect of being able to obtain as many horses shortly as would enable us to prosecute our voyage by land should that by water be deemed unadvisable.

   _____

   _____

"The Fall of the House of Usher" and **"The Raven"** by Edgar Allan Poe

Literary Analysis: Single Effect and Style

Edgar Allan Poe believed that a short story should be constructed to achieve a "certain unique or **single effect.**" In "The Fall of the House of Usher," every aspect of the author's **style** contributes to and heightens the single effect. These elements of style include choice of words, length of sentences, type and structure of sentences, rhythm, and literary devices.

DIRECTIONS: Read this passage from "The Fall of the House of Usher." Explain how each element of style contributes to the story's single effect.

> It was, especially, upon retiring to bed late in the night of the seventh or eighth day after the placing of the lady Madeline within the donjon, that I experienced the full power of such feelings. Sleep came not near my couch—while the hours waned and waned away. I struggled to reason off the nervousness which had dominion over me. I endeavored to believe that much, if not all of what I felt, was due to the bewildering influence of the gloomy furniture of the room—of the dark and tattered draperies, which, tortured into motion by the breath of a rising tempest, swayed fitfully to and fro upon the walls, and rustled uneasily about the decorations of the bed.

1. Does the author choose simple and direct words or words that are more complex and formal? How does this contribute to the story's single effect?

   _____

   _____

   _____

2. List at least three examples of word choices that help contribute to the story's single effect.

   _____

   _____

   _____

3. How does sentence length and structure contribute to the story's single effect?

   _____

   _____

   _____

4. List at least two examples of how the author creates an internal rhythm by repeating words or ideas from sentence to sentence. How does this contribute to the single effect?

   _____

   _____

   _____

5. Does the author use vivid imagery or strong similes, metaphors, or other literary devices? How does this contribute to the story's single effect?

   _____

   _____

   _____

Unit 3: A Growing Nation (1800–1870)

Name _____ Date _____

"The Minister's Black Veil" by Nathaniel Hawthorne

Literary Analysis: Setting and Allegory

An **allegory** is a literary work in which characters, events, settings, and other story elements have symbolic meaning. In "The Minister's Black Veil," the black veil serves as the central symbol of the sins of humanity.

Individual elements within the work also have symbolic meanings. One element that contributes to the symbolic meaning in an allegory is the **setting,** or the particular time and place in which the tale occurs. Setting includes details that fall into several categories, such as location, weather, geography, time of day, season, and atmosphere. Social and economic conditions are also an important aspect of a story's setting.

DIRECTIONS: Read these passages from "The Minister's Black Veil." Each describes a setting. Explain what each setting symbolizes in the context of the story and how it contributes to the allegory as a whole.

1. The old people of the village came stooping along the street. Children, with bright faces, tripped merrily beside their parents, or mimicked a graver gait, in the conscious dignity of their Sunday clothes. Spruce bachelors looked sidelong at the pretty maidens, and fancied that the Sabbath sunshine made them prettier than on weekdays.

   _____

   _____

2. When Mr. Hooper came, the first thing that their eyes rested on was the same horrible black veil, which had added deeper gloom to the funeral, and could portend nothing but evil to the wedding. Such was its immediate effect on the guests that a cloud seemed to have rolled duskily from beneath the black crape, and dimmed the light of the candles.

   _____

   _____

3. And there lay the hoary head of good Father Hooper upon the death pillow, with the black veil still swathed about his brow, and reaching down over his face, so that each more difficult gasp of his faint breath caused it to stir. All through life that piece of crape had hung between him and the world; it had separated him from cheerful brotherhood and woman's love and kept him in that saddest of all prisons, his own heart; and still it lay upon his face, as if to deepen the gloom of his darksome chamber, and shade him from the sunshine of eternity.

   _____

   _____

4. The grass of many years has sprung up and withered on that grave, the burial stone is moss-grown, and good Mr. Hooper's face is dust; but awful is still the thought that it moldered beneath the Black Veil!

   _____

   _____

Name _____ Date _____

from _Moby-Dick_ by Herman Melville

Literary Analysis: Comparing Symbols

A **symbol** is a person, place, action, or thing that also represents an abstract meaning beyond itself. Authors use symbols to help them express themes. Symbols of nature appear in many works of literature. Sometimes, these symbols have similar meanings; sometimes they are different. You can compare the meanings that different authors associate with different symbols from nature.

For example, you might compare Herman Melville's use of the whale as a symbol in _Moby-Dick_ with Edgar Allan Poe's use of the raven as a symbol in "The Raven." To compare the two symbols, consider similarities and differences. For example, Melville frequently stresses Moby Dick's white color, while Poe stresses the raven's blackness. White often symbolizes purity and good. Melville also compares the white color to blankness, emphasizing the impartiality of nature. Black is often a symbol of evil or despair; the raven comes to symbolize the narrator's madness and loss.

DIRECTIONS: Compare Edgar Allan Poe's use of the raven as a symbol in "The Raven" with Melville's use of the whale as a symbol in _Moby-Dick_.

1. How does the narrator of the poem relate to the raven? How is his attitude similar to Ahab's attitude toward the whale?

   _____

   _____

   _____

2. How might both the raven and the whale be considered unnatural?

   _____

   _____

   _____

3. Why do you think both authors choose an animal as a central symbol? What aspects of nature can animals represent that other parts of nature cannot?

   _____

   _____

   _____

4. How would you summarize the symbolic similarities between the raven and the whale?

   _____

   _____

   _____

5. How would you summarize the symbolic differences between the raven and the whale?

   _____

   _____

   _____

from *Nature*, from *Self-Reliance*, "The Snowstorm," and "Concord Hymn"
by Ralph Waldo Emerson

Literary Analysis: Personification and Transcendentalism

When writers give human powers and characteristics to something that is not human, such as an object, an aspect of nature, or an idea, they're using **personification.** This device is often used by transcendental writers. Remember that one of the fundamental principles of **transcendentalism** is that the human spirit is reflected in nature. Writers can personify nature to emphasize this connection. For example, Emerson opens "The Snowstorm" with this description:

> Announced by all the trumpets of the sky,
> Arrives the snow, and, driving o'er the fields,
> Seems nowhere to alight…

The storm is personified as a person driving across fields, stopping nowhere.

DIRECTIONS: Answer the following questions to identify and analyze Emerson's use of personification.

1. What is being personified in this excerpt from *Nature?*

   The greatest delight which the fields and woods minister is the suggestion of an occult relation between man and the vegetable. I am not alone and unacknowledged. They nod to me, and I to them.

   _____

2. What is personified in this excerpt, and how?

   For nature is not always tricked in holiday attire, but the same scene which yesterday breathed perfume and glittered as for the frolic of the nymphs is overspread with melancholy today.

   _____

3. Why do you think Emerson uses personification in this essay?

   _____

   _____

   _____

4. What is being personified in these lines from "The Snowstorm"?

   Come see the north wind's masonry.
   Out of an unseen quarry evermore
   Furnished with tile, the fierce artificer
   Curves his white bastions with projected roof
   Round every windward stake, or tree, or door.

   _____

5. How does the use of personification in "The Snowstorm" help show Emerson's belief in transcendentalism?

   _____

   _____

from *Walden* and from *Civil Disobedience* by Henry David Thoreau

Literary Analysis: Recognizing Styles

Each writer has a unique **style**, or way of putting thoughts into words. As you become familiar with an author's writing, you begin to recognize his or her style. For example, after reading excerpts from *Walden* and *Civil Disobedience*, you might make these generalizations about Thoreau's style:

- He builds his paragraphs to a climax.
- He uses a variety of sentence types.
- He creates rhythms by repeating words and creating parallel phrases.

Just as you can sometimes recognize what singer is performing a song that you have never heard, you can sometimes recognize an author by his or her style.

DIRECTIONS: Read the paragraphs. One is by Emerson; the other is by Thoreau. Review the essays you have read by these authors. Complete the chart to help you assign authorship.

Paragraph A: But if a man would be alone, let him look at the stars. The rays that come from those heavenly worlds will separate between him and what he touches. One might think the atmosphere was made transparent with this design, to give man, in the heavenly bodies, the perpetual presence of the sublime. Seen in the streets of cities, how great they are! If the stars should appear one night in a thousand years, how would men believe and adore; and preserve for many generations the remembrance of the city of God which had been shown! But every night come out these envoys of beauty, and light the universe with their admonishing smile.

Paragraph B: I see young men, my townsmen, whose misfortune it is to have inherited farms, houses, barns, cattle, and farming tools; for these are more easily acquired than got rid of. Better if they had been born in the open pasture and suckled by a wolf, that they might have seen with clearer eyes what field they were called to labor in. Who made them serfs of the soil? Why should they eat their sixty acres, when man is condemned to eat only his peck of dirt? Why should they begin digging their graves as soon as they are born?

	Paragraph A	Paragraph B
1. **Number of sentences**		
2. **Number of words**		
3. **Average sentence length**		
4. **Number of statements**		
5. **Number of questions**		
6. **Number of exclamations**		

7. I believe that Paragraph A is by _____ because _____

_____

_____

8. I believe that Paragraph B is by _____ because _____

_____

_____

Unit 3: A Growing Nation (1800–1870)

Name _____ Date _____

Emily Dickinson's Poetry

Literary Analysis: Stanzas and Rhyme Patterns

A **stanza** is a group of lines in a poem that is considered to be a unit. Stanzas often function like a paragraph. Each stanza states and develops a single main idea. Rhyme patterns, or schemes, often repeat from one stanza to the next, giving the poem unity. Emily Dickinson often uses slant rhymes as part of the rhyme pattern in her stanzas.

For example, Emily Dickinson writes this poem in one stanza:

Water, is taught by thirst,	a
Land—by the Oceans passed.	a
Transport—by throe—	b
Peace—by its battles told—	c
Love, by Memorial Mold—	c
Birds, by the Snow.	b

The letters at the right indicate the rhyme pattern. The first two lines end with slant rhymes; the third and sixth lines end with exact rhymes, as do the fourth and fifth lines.

Analyzing the stanza structure can help you focus on the poet's meaning. Dickinson writes "Water, is taught by thirst" in one stanza because it presents one main idea about how we use opposites and comparisons to understand our world.

DIRECTIONS: Read each of the following stanzas. Describe the form of the stanza, including its number of lines and rhyming pattern. Then summarize the stanza's main idea.

1. The Brain—is wider than the Sky—
   For—put them side by side—
   The one the other will contain
   With ease—and You—beside—

   Stanza form: _____

   Summary: _____

   _____

2. My life closed twice before its close—
   It yet remains to see
   If Immortality unveil
   A third event to me.

   Stanza form: _____

   Summary: _____

   _____

3. The Soul selects her own Society—
   Then—shuts the Door—
   To her divine Majority—
   Present no more—

   Stanza form: _____

   Summary: _____

   _____

Walt Whitman's Poetry

Literary Analysis: Comparing Ideas and Ways of Expressing Them

Whitman, Emerson, and Thoreau expressed some similar ideas, though they used different forms of writing. You can compare ideas expressed in free verse with those presented in prose. For example, compare Whitman's free verse description of looking at a blade of grass with Emerson's thoughts while standing in the woods.

I loaf and invite my soul,
I lean and loaf at my ease, observing a spear of summer grass.

My tongue, every atom of my blood, formed from this soil, this air…

—Whitman, "Song of Myself"

Standing on the bare ground—my head bathed by the blithe air and uplifted into infinite space—all mean egotism vanishes. I become a transparent eyeball; I am nothing; I see all; the currents of the Universal Being circulate through me; I am part or parcel of God.

—Emerson, *Nature*

Both writers express the feeling that they are at one with nature. They both share an attitude of exuberant joy at the wonders of observing and interacting with nature.

DIRECTIONS: Compare each pair of quotations. How are they alike in content? How do they differ in form?

A foolish consistency is the hobgoblin of little minds, adored by little statesmen and philosophers and divines. With consistency a great soul has simply nothing to do. He may as well concern himself with his shadow on the wall. Speak what you think now in hard words and tomorrow speak what tomorrow thinks in hard words again, though it contradict everything you said today.

—Emerson, *Self-Reliance*

Do I contradict myself?
Very well then I contradict myself,
(I am large, I contain multitudes.)

—Whitman, "Song of Myself"

1. _____

   _____

I went to the woods because I wished to live deliberately, to front only the essential facts of life, and see if I could not learn what it had to teach, and not, when I came to die, discover that I had not lived.

—Thoreau, *Walden*

I am enamor'd of growing outdoors,
Of men that live among cattle or taste of the ocean or woods,
Of the builders and steerers of ships…
I can eat and sleep with them week in and week out.

—Whitman, "Song of Myself"

2. _____

   _____

Unit 3: A Growing Nation (1800–1870)

"An Episode of War" by Stephen Crane
"Willie Has Gone to the War," words by George Cooper, music by Stephen Foster

Literary Analysis: Comparison of Realism and Naturalism

Realism is an approach to literature in which the writer tries to show people and their lives as realistically as possible. Realistic literature focuses on ordinary people rather than on extraordinary ones. It shows real behavior rather than model behavior. It often emphasizes the harsh realities of ordinary people's lives.

Naturalism expands on the base begun in realism. Writers who create naturalistic literature also present realistic people rather than romanticized characters. However, they add the ideas that people's lives are often deeply affected by natural forces such as heredity, environment, political situations, or even chance.

The main contrast between the two movements is that naturalism emphasizes the lack of control its realistic characters have over the changes taking place in their lives. Elements of both realism and naturalism can often be seen in the same piece of literature, such as "An Episode of War" by Stephen Crane.

DIRECTIONS: Use details from "An Episode of War" and "Willie Has Gone to the War" to compare and contrast the uses of realism and naturalism in the two texts.

1. Tell how "An Episode of War" reflects realism by presenting ordinary people instead of extraordinary ones.

   _____

   _____

   _____

2. Tell how "Willie Has Gone to War" reflects realism by presenting ordinary people instead of extraordinary ones.

   _____

   _____

   _____

3. Tell how "An Episode of War" emphasizes an individual's lack of control over his or her own destiny.

   _____

   _____

   _____

4. Tell how "Willie Goes to War" emphasizes an individual's lack of control over his or her own destiny.

   _____

   _____

   _____

5. Compare and contrast the use of realism and naturalism in both pieces.

   _____

   _____

Name _____ Date _____

Literary Analysis: Allegory and Refrain

A **refrain** is a word, phrase, line, or group of lines repeated at regular intervals. In spirituals, refrains emphasize the most important ideas. In "Go Down, Moses," for example, the refrain "Let my people go" is repeated seven times. The constant repetition serves to turn the cry for freedom into a demand. An **allegory** has two levels of meaning, a literal level and a symbolic level. Spirituals from the period of slavery often have elements of allegory. They typically deal with religious freedom, and, allegorically, with political freedom.

DIRECTIONS: Underline the refrains in these stanzas from the spirituals. Then answer the questions to identify the two levels of meaning in the stanzas.

"Swing Low, Sweet Chariot"

Swing low, sweet chariot,	I looked over Jordan and what did I see
Coming for to carry me home,	Coming for to carry me home,
Swing low, sweet chariot,	A band of angels coming after me,
Coming for to carry me home.	Coming for to carry me home.

1. What are the literal meanings of the two refrains in the first stanza? What are the symbolic meanings?

   _____

   _____

2. What are the two levels of meaning in the second stanza?

   _____

   _____

   _____

3. How does the refrain in the second stanza emphasize the meaning of the other lines?

   _____

   _____

"Go Down, Moses"

Go down, Moses,	"Thus saith the Lord," bold Moses said,
Way down in Egypt land	"Let my people go;
Tell old Pharaoh	If not I'll smite your first-born dead
"Let my people go."	Let my people go."

4. How do both stanzas illustrate the literal meaning of the refrain "Let my people go"?

   _____

   _____

5. What is the symbolic meaning of the refrain "Let my people go"?

   _____

   _____

from *My Bondage and My Freedom* by Frederick Douglass

Literary Analysis: Comparing Autobiographies

In his autobiography, Frederick Douglass conveys facts about slavery, but he also tells a story, makes judgments, and communicates feelings. Through the use of a narrative, he lends power to the statements he is making about slavery.

DIRECTIONS: Read the first passage, which is from Douglass's autobiography. Then read the passage from *The Autobiography* by Benjamin Franklin. Answer the questions that follow.

It is due, however, to my mistress to say, that she did not adopt this course in all its stringency at the first. She either thought it unnecessary, or she lacked the depravity indispensable to shutting me up in mental darkness. It was, at least, necessary for her to have some training, and some hardening, in the exercise of the slaveholder's prerogative, to make her equal to forgetting my human nature and character, and to treating me as a thing destitute of a moral or an intellectual nature.

—Frederick Douglass

While my care was employed in guarding against one fault, I was often surprised by another. …I concluded, at length, that the mere speculative conviction that it was our interest to be completely virtuous was not sufficient to prevent our slipping; and that the contrary habits must be broken, and good ones acquired and established, before we can have any dependence on a steady, uniform rectitude of conduct.

—Benjamin Franklin

1. Besides being autobiographical, what do these passages have in common? Think about the subjects treated in each passage.

   _____

   _____

   _____

   _____

   _____

2. Which passage does a better job of telling a story? Explain your answer.

   _____

   _____

   _____

   _____

3. In what ways are these two examples of autobiographical writing different?

   _____

   _____

   _____

   _____

4. Which passage do you find more interesting? Explain your answer.

   _____

   _____

"An Occurrence at Owl Creek Bridge" by Ambrose Bierce

Literary Analysis: Description and Point of View

A writer's choice about which point of view to use has many effects on the story told. It not only decides what the reader will and will not learn, but it also influences whether the reader feels close to or far away from the action. The choice of point of view also affects the **descriptions,** the writing that captures the senses of sight, sound, smell, taste, and physical feeling or sensation.

DIRECTIONS: Underline the descriptions in the following passages from "An Occurrence at Owl Creek Bridge." To the right, indicate the sense to which each description appeals. Then rewrite each passage from the point of view indicated, altering some descriptions to accommodate that point of view.

1. Then all at once, with a terrible suddenness, the light about him shot upward with the noise of a loud plash; a frightful roaring was in his ears, and all was cold and dark. The power of thought was restored; he knew that the rope had broken and he had fallen into the stream.

_____
_____
_____
_____

First-person point of view:

_____
_____
_____
_____

2. A counterswirl had caught Farquhar and turned him half round; he was again looking into the forest on the bank opposite the fort. The sound of a clear, high voice in a monotonous singsong now rang out behind him and came across the water with a distinctness that pierced and subdued all other sounds, even the beating of the ripples in his ears.

_____
_____
_____
_____
_____

Third-person omniscient point of view:

_____
_____
_____
_____

Unit 4: Division, Reconciliation, and Expansion (1850–1914)

Name _____ Date _____

"The Gettysburg Address" and **"Second Inaugural Address"** by Abraham Lincoln
"Letter to His Son" by Robert E. Lee

Literary Analysis: Diction and Style

Diction, which is word choice, gives the writer's voice its unique quality. The writer's diction reflects the audience and purpose of the work. For example, speeches are generally formal, and letters tend to be informal. Diction is one element of an author's **style.** Style includes word choice, length of sentences, structure of sentences, and rhythm.

DIRECTIONS: Read each of the following passages. Answer the questions about the writer's style and how the style affects the audience and the purpose. Then determine whether each one is a speech or a letter.

> To strengthen, perpetuate, and extend this interest was the object for which the insurgents would rend the Union, even by war; while the government claimed no right to do more than to restrict the territorial enlargement of it. Neither party expected for the war, the magnitude, or the duration, which it has already attained.

1. Describe the word choices and sentence structure. Are they better suited to an audience of one person or many? Explain.

   _____

   _____

   _____

2. Describe the rhythm of the passage. Would you rather read this passage or hear it? Why?

   _____

   _____

   _____

3. Is this a letter or a speech? _____

> The South, in my opinion, has been aggrieved by the acts of the North, as you say. I feel the aggression and am willing to take every proper step for redress. It is the principle I contend for, not individual or private benefit. As an American citizen, I take great pride in my country, her prosperity and institutions, and would defend any state if her rights were invaded.

4. Describe the word choices and sentence structure. Are they better suited to an audience of one person or many? Explain.

   _____

   _____

   _____

5. Describe the rhythm of the passage. Would you rather read this passage or hear it? Why?

   _____

   _____

   _____

6. Is this a letter or a speech? _____

from Civil War Diaries, Journals, and Letters

Literary Analysis: Comparing Diaries, Journals, and Letters

Diaries, journals, and **letters** are three types of private, personal writings that often reveal the writer's thoughts and feelings. Often you can understand a diary, journal, or letter writer's personal views, feelings, and personality more fully by comparing and contrasting his or her writings with those of another person.

DIRECTIONS: Answer each question using information from the passages and what you know about diaries, journals, and letters.

1. Mary Chesnut writes: I sprang out of bed. And on my knees—prostrate—I prayed as I had never prayed before.

   Warren Lee Goss writes: With a nervous tremor convulsing my system, and my heart thumping like muffled drumbeats, I stood before the door of the recruiting office…

   What similar feeling do the two writers express in these passages? Which writer do you feel expresses the feeling in a more personal and revealing way? Why?

   _____

   _____

2. Randolph McKim writes: Its ranks had been sadly thinned, and its energies greatly depleted by those six fearful hours of battle that morning; but its nerve and spirit were undiminished.

   Stonewall Jackson writes: My preservation was entirely due, as was the glorious victory, to our God, to whom be all the honor, praise and glory.

   Both writers are describing the aftermath of battle. How are their descriptions similar or different? What does each description reflect about the writer?

   _____

   _____

   _____

   _____

3. Reverend Henry M. Turner writes: The President came to the window and made responsive bows, and thousands told him, if he would come out of that palace, they would hug him to death. …

   Mary Chesnut writes: Lincoln or Seward have made such silly advances and then far sillier drawings back.

   Both writers refer to President Lincoln in their statements. How do their attitudes toward the president differ?

   _____

   _____

   _____

Name _____   Date _____

"The Boys' Ambition" from *Life on the Mississippi* and "The Notorious Jumping Frog of Calaveras County" by Mark Twain

Literary Analysis: Irony in Humor

Humor in literature is intended to evoke laughter. Much humor stems from **irony**—a situation in which the opposite of what you expect is said or done. It is this ironic unexpectedness that makes you laugh.

DIRECTIONS: For each passage, explain how irony plays a part in the humor. Tell what is unexpected in the statement or observation that evokes laughter.

1. …now and then we had a hope that if we lived and were good, God would permit us to be pirates.

   This is ironic because you do not expect _____

   _____

   _____

   _____

2. When his boat blew up at last, it diffused a tranquil contentment among us such as we had not known for months.

   This is ironic because you do not expect _____

   _____

   _____

   _____

3. The minister's son became an engineer. The doctor's and the postmaster's sons became mud clerks…

   _____

   _____

   _____

4. …I had comforting daydreams of a future when I should be a great and honored pilot, with plenty of money, and could kill some of these mates and clerks and pay for them.

   This is ironic because you do not expect _____

   _____

   _____

   _____

5. "What might it be that you've got in the box?"
   And Smiley says, sorter indifferent-like, 'It might be a parrot, or it might be a canary, maybe, but it ain't—it's only just a frog.'

   This is ironic because you do not expect _____

   _____

   _____

   _____

"The Outcasts of Poker Flat" by Bret Harte

Literary Analysis: Comparing Regionalism

Regionalism is a type of literature that attempts to capture the "local color" of a region by showing the distinctive qualities of its inhabitants and its physical environment. This is often accomplished by accurately representing local customs, attitudes, and speech patterns, as well as a description of the unique environment.

DIRECTIONS: Compare elements of regionalism in these passages from Harte's "The Outcasts of Poker Flat" and Twain's *Life on the Mississippi.*

It was one of the peculiarities of that mountain climate that its rays diffused a kindly warmth over the wintry landscape, as if in regretful commiseration of the past. But it revealed drift on drift of snow piled high around the hut—a hopeless, uncharted, trackless sea of white lying below the rocky shores to which the castaways still clung. Through the marvelously clear air the smoke of the pastoral village of Poker Flat rose miles away. Mother Shipton saw it, and from a remote pinnacle of her rocky fastness hurled in that direction a final malediction. It was her last vituperative attempt, and perhaps for that reason was invested with a certain degree of sublimity. It did her good, she privately informed the Duchess. "Just you go out there and cuss, and see."

—"The Outcasts of Poker Flat"

After all these years I can picture that old time to myself now, just as it was then: the white town drowsing in the sunshine of a summer's morning… one or two clerks sitting in front of the Water Street stores, with their splint-bottomed chairs tilted back against the wall, chins on breasts, hats slouched over their faces, asleep… the great Mississippi, the majestic, the magnificent Mississippi, rolling its mile-wide tide along, shining in the sun; the dense forest away on the other side; the point above the town, and the point below, bounding the river-glimpse and turning it into a sort of sea, and withal a very still and brilliant and lonely one. Presently a film of dark smoke appears above one of those remote points; instantly a Negro drayman, famous for his quick eye and prodigious voice, lifts up the cry, "S-t-e-a-m-boat a-comin'!"

—"Life on the Mississippi"

	The Outcasts of Poker Flat	Life on the Mississippi
1. **Setting**		
2. **Characters**		
3. **Dialogue**		

Literary Analysis for Enrichment   **31**

Name _____ Date _____

"Heading West" by Miriam Colt David
"I Will Fight No More Forever" by Chief Joseph

Literary Analysis: Comparing Tone

The **tone** of a literary work is the writer's attitude toward the subject, characters, events, or audience. Nonfiction writers use descriptive words and details to suggest tone. Often, tone can be described with adjectives such as *humorous, ironic, fearful, cheerful,* or *angry.*

DIRECTIONS: Compare the tones in the passages from "Heading West" and "I Will Fight No More Forever." List details from each passage that help establish the tone. Then identify the tone of each passage. Finally, explain what is similar and what is different about the tones of the passages.

Can anyone imagine our disappointment this morning, on learning from this and that member, that no mills have been built; that the directors, after receiving our money to build mills, have not fulfilled the trust reposed in them, and that in consequence, some families have already left the settlement…?

As it is, we find the families, some living in tents of cloth, some of cloth and green bark just peeled from the trees, and some wholly of green bark, stuck up on the damp ground, without floors or fires. Only two stoves in the company…

—"Heading West"

The little children are freezing to death. My people, some of them, have run away to the hills and have no blankets, no food; no one knows where they are—perhaps freezing to death. I want to have time to look for my children and see how many I can find. Maybe I shall find them among the dead. Hear me, my chiefs. I am tired; my heart is sick and sad.

—"I Will Fight No More Forever"

	Heading West	**I Will Fight No More Forever**
Details		
Tone		

Similar _____

Different _____

"**To Build a Fire**" by Jack London

Literary Analysis: Comparing Characters' Conflicts

Conflict is the struggle between two opposing forces. In an **internal conflict,** a character struggles with a problem within himself or herself. In an **external conflict,** a character strug-gles against an outside force, such as another character or nature.

DIRECTIONS: Think about the different conflicts that existed for each set of characters. Explain how the conflicts are similar or different.

1. Explain how the external conflict of the man in "To Light a Fire" is similar to the external conflict faced by the characters in "The Outcasts of Poker Flat."

   _____

   _____

   _____

   _____

   _____

2. Explain how the external conflict of the man in "To Light a Fire" is different from the external conflict faced by the characters in "The Outcasts of Poker Flat."

   _____

   _____

   _____

   _____

   _____

3. Explain how the external conflict of the man in "To Light a Fire" is similar to and different from the external conflict faced by Miriam Davis Colt in "Heading West."

   _____

   _____

   _____

   _____

4. Explain how the conflict faced by Chief Joseph in "I Will Fight No More Forever" is both similar to and different from the conflict faced by the man in "To Light a Fire."

   _____

   _____

   _____

   _____

Unit 4: Division, Reconciliation, and Expansion (1850–1914)

"The Story of an Hour" by Kate Chopin

Literary Analysis: Irony and Plot

Irony is a contrast between what is stated in a literary work and what is meant, or between what is expected to happen and what actually does happen. Often, irony is generated by the events that take place in a literary work, or its **plot.** The plot of a story usually has five elements: the exposition, or introduction; the rising action; the climax, or high point of interest; the falling action; and the resolution.

There are two kinds of irony that are affected by plot.

- In **situational irony**, the outcome of an action or situation contradicts the expectations of the characters, reader, or audience.

  She said it over and over under her breath: "free, free, free!"

  The reader is surprised that Mrs. Mallard is happy to learn that her husband is dead.

- In **dramatic irony**, readers are aware of something that a character does not know.

  "Louise, open the door! I beg; open the door—you will make yourself ill."

  Readers know that Mrs. Mallard is happy, not despondent.

DIRECTIONS: Fill in this plot chart with ironic incidents that occur for each element of the plot. Identify each incident as situational irony or dramatic irony.

Plot Element	Ironic Incident	Type of Irony
1. **Exposition**	Mrs. Mallard's "heart condition" is established, though readers later realize that she is not frail and delicate.	situational and dramatic
2. **Rising action**		
3. **Climax**		
4. **Falling action**		
5. **Resolution**		

Name _____ Date _____

Literary Analysis: Elements of Plot—Rising Action

Rising action is the stage of plot development that follows the exposition and ends with the climax. It is the stage in which complications arise and tensions build. The main characters may run into difficulties, and the conflict can become more difficult to resolve. In this section of "April Showers," the character of Theodora must grapple with her twin desires—the hope of becoming a published author and the desire to fulfill her obligations to her family.

DIRECTIONS: As you read "April Showers," use the chart to analyze the rising action. In the left column, list several of the events that make up the rising action. In the right column, describe how each event heightens suspense for the reader and creates complications for the characters.

Event	How Event Creates Complications and Builds Suspense

Unit 4: Division, Reconciliation, and Expansion (1850–1914)

"Douglass" and **"We Wear the Mask"** by Paul Laurence Dunbar

Literary Analysis: Rhyme and Meter

Rhyme is the repetition of sounds in the accented syllables of two or more words appearing close to each other. A rhyme that occurs at the end of a line is called an **end rhyme.** A **rhyme scheme** is a pattern of end rhymes in a poem. To describe a rhyme scheme, use a letter to represent each rhyming sound.

Meter is the rhythmic pattern of accented (´) and unaccented (˘) syllables in a line of poetry. The basic unit of meter is the **foot**—one accented syllable and one or more unaccented syllables. An **iamb** is a foot with one unaccented syllable followed by an accented syllable. A line of **iambic tetrameter** is a line with *four* iambic feet. To describe the meter of a poem, mark the accented and unaccented syllables, with lines between the feet:

We wear / the mask / that grins / and lies,

DIRECTIONS: Answer each question to analyze the rhyme and meter of "We Wear the Mask."

1. What is the rhyme scheme in the poem?

   _____

2. a. Which lines are in iambic tetrameter?

   _____

   b. Which lines are not in iambic tetrameter?

   _____

3. What effect does the use of rhyme and meter have? How does it contribute to the meaning of the poem?

   _____

   _____

   _____

   _____

   _____

   _____

"Luke Havergal" and **"Richard Cory"** by Edwin Arlington Robinson
"Lucinda Matlock" and **"Richard Bone"** by Edgar Lee Masters

Literary Analysis: Comparing Speakers

The **speaker** is the voice of the poem. Often the speaker is the poet, but the speaker may also be a fictional character or even a nonhuman being. The speaker affects what you are told and how you are told it.

DIRECTIONS: Answer these questions about the poems by Edwin Arlington Robinson and Edgar Lee Masters.

1. a. Who is the speaker in "Luke Havergal"? _____

   b. in "Richard Cory"? _____

   c. in "Lucinda Matlock"? _____

   d. in "Richard Bone"? _____

2. How might the poem "Luke Havergal" be affected if the speaker were Luke himself?

   _____

   _____

   _____

3. How might the poem "Richard Cory" be affected if the speaker were Richard himself?

   _____

   _____

   _____

4. How might the poem "Lucinda Matlock" be affected if the speaker were another character in the town?

   _____

   _____

   _____

5. How might the poem "Richard Bone" be affected if the speaker were a spirit?

   _____

   _____

   _____

Unit 4: Division, Reconciliation, and Expansion (1850–1914)

Name _____ Date _____

"A Wagner Matinée" by Willa Cather

Literary Analysis: Comparing Characterizations

Characterization is the means by which a writer reveals a character's personality. Writers generally develop character through one of the following methods:

- direct statements about the character

- physical descriptions of the character

- actions, thoughts, and comments of the character

- comments about the character made by other characters

DIRECTIONS: Compare and contrast the characterizations of Aunt Georgiana in "A Wagner Matinée" and those of Lucinda Matlock in "Lucinda Matlock". Complete this chart with details and lines from the selections.

Character Trait	Aunt Georgiana	Lucinda Matlock
1. **Home and type of work**		
2. **Family**		
3. **Age and physical appearance**		
4. **Level of sophistication/ love of arts**		
5. **Hardworking**		
6. **Contentment with life?**		

"The Love Song of J. Alfred Prufrock" by T. S. Eliot

Literary Analysis: Comparing Poems

Two of the most celebrated American poems are T. S. Eliot's "The Love Song of J. Alfred Prufrock" and Walt Whitman's "Song of Myself". Each poem provides a distinct portrait of both a person and a time in history. "Song of Myself" celebrates America at a time when it was still a predominantly rural and agricultural nation. "The Love Song of J. Alfred Prufrock" comments on modern life at a time when the urban center has become its focus.

DIRECTIONS: Read the "The Love Song of J. Alfred Prufrock" and the excerpts from "Song of Myself." Answer the questions that follow.

1. Compare the depiction of nature and rural life in "Song of Myself" with the depiction of urban life in "The Love Song of J. Alfred Prufrock." Provide examples of the types of descriptive images each poet uses.

   _____

   _____

   _____

   _____

   _____

2. Contrast the personalities of each poem's speaker. Would Whitman's speaker every wonder "Do I dare?" Would Eliot's speaker ever proclaim "I celebrate myself, and sing myself"?

   _____

   _____

   _____

   _____

   _____

   _____

   _____

3. Describe each speaker's feelings toward other people.

   _____

   _____

   _____

   _____

   _____

4. What do you think Whitman's speaker and Prufrock would think of each other if they met?

   _____

   _____

   _____

Imagist Poets

Literary Analysis: Comparing Poetic Styles

Imagist poems evoke emotion and spark the reader's imagination through the vivid presentation of a limited number of images. They contain everyday language, precise words, and concrete images. They avoid clichés and suggest meaning rather than stating it directly. Imagist poems are written in free verse, since one of the poets' objectives is to create new rhythms.

DIRECTIONS: Compare and contrast this imagist poem "The Great Figure" by William Carlos Williams with "My life closed twice before its close—" by Emily Dickenson. Answer the questions below.

"The Great Figure"

Among the rain
and lights
I saw the figure 5
in gold
on a red
fire truck
moving
tense
unheeded
to gong clangs
siren howls
and wheels rumbling
through the dark city.

"My life closed twice before its close—"

My life closed twice before its close—
It yet remains to see
If immortality unveil
A third event to me.

So huge, so hopeless to conceive
As these that twice befell.
Parting is all we know of heaven.
And all we need of hell.

1. What are the subjects of the two poems?

   _____

   _____

   _____

2. What concrete images can you find in Williams's poem? In Dickinson's poem?

   _____

   _____

   _____

   _____

3. How do the rhythms of the poems differ?

   _____

   _____

   _____

4. Do you think these two poems state meaning or suggest it? Explain.

   _____

   _____

   _____

Name _____ Date _____

"Winter Dreams" by F. Scott Fitzgerald

Literary Analysis: Characterization and Short Stories

Characterization is an important part of most short stories. Some short stories revolve almost entirely around the thoughts, feelings, and actions of a main character or characters. Such short stories are said to be "character-driven" because they turn on the personal qualities of the characters. "Winter Dreams" is an example of a character-driven short story.

DIRECTIONS: Review the characters in "Winter Dreams." Then answer the questions.

1. In character-driven short stories, the action revolves around the story's main character or characters. Who are these characters in "Winter Dreams"?

_____

_____

2. What is the main conflict of "Winter Dreams"? Is it internal or external? Which character or characters does it involve?

_____

_____

_____

3. How are the characters in "Winter Dreams" transformed by the end of the story?

_____

_____

_____

_____

4. Name two of your favorite short stories from your reading so far and explain why you like them. Are they character-driven? Discuss the appeal character-driven stories have for you. List the limitations that character-driven stories have for you.

_____

_____

_____

_____

_____

_____

_____

_____

_____

_____

_____

_____

Name _____ Date _____

"The Turtle" from *The Grapes of Wrath* by John Steinbeck

Literary Analysis: Comparing Themes

The **theme** in a literary work is the central message its author expresses about life. An author's theme is shown through story events, characters, and even story details. Although a theme usually comments on the human experience, it is not stated explicitly, and such a message can be expressed even in works that feature nonhuman characters.

DIRECTIONS: John Steinbeck's "The Turtle" and Walt Whitman's "A Noiseless Patient Spider" use nonhuman living characters to make statements about the human experience. Review these two works and answer the questions that follow.

1. How does Whitman use nonhuman characters to comment on the human experience?

_____

_____

_____

2. How does Steinbeck use nonhuman characters to comment on the human experience?

_____

_____

_____

3. Which work is more concerned with life's spiritual aspects? Explain.

_____

_____

_____

4. Which work is more concerned with life's physical aspects? Explain.

_____

_____

_____

5. What attitude toward nature is expressed by each author?

Whitman: _____

_____

Steinbeck: _____

_____

Both: _____

_____

_____

_____

_____

"anyone lived in a pretty how town" and **"old age sticks"** by E. E. Cummings
"The Unknown Citizen" by W. H. Auden

Literary Analysis: Satire and Poetic Structure

Satire is writing in which an author uses humor to ridicule or criticize certain individuals, institutions, types of behavior, or even humanity. Satire can even be expressed by the structure of a piece of literature. In the poems "anyone lived in a pretty how town," "old age sticks," and "The Unknown Citizen," the poetic structure is part of the satire. For instance, the broken syntax of the words in stanza four of "old age sticks" is one way Cummings ridicules the feeble nature of old age's protests.

DIRECTIONS: Read the excerpts and then answer the questions that follow.

> He was fully sensible to the advantages of the Installment Plan
> And had everything necessary to the Modern Man...

1. Why is this rhyme satirical?

   _____

   _____

   _____

   _____

> That, in the modern sense of an old-fashioned word, he was a saint,
> For in everything he did he served the Greater Community.

2. Why is it satirical to capitalize "Greater Community"?

   _____

   _____

   _____

> children guessed (but only a few
> and down they forgot as up they grew

3. How is the unconventional syntax in these lines part of the satire about growing up?

   _____

   _____

   _____

> youth yanks them
> down(old
> age
> cries No

4. How are the parentheses and lack of punctuation part of Cummings's satirical critique of youth's attitude toward old age?

   _____

   _____

   _____

Unit 5: Disillusion, Defiance, and Discontent (1914–1946)

Name _____ Date _____

"The Far and the Near" by Thomas Wolfe

Literary Analysis: Comparing Climax and Anticlimax

Most short stories have plots based on a similar structure: exposition, rising action, climax, falling action, resolution. The high point of a story is its **climax.** If a story has been compelling, the writer has built up expectations about the outcome, and the climax should fulfill those expectations. If the author builds up the reader's expectations only to disappoint them, the story is said to have an **anticlimax.**

DIRECTIONS: Use the following questions to compare and contrast the plot structures of "The Far and the Near" and "To Build a Fire".

1. Summarize the **exposition** of each story. Then describe the central issue or **conflict.**
   "The Far and the Near": _____
   _____
   _____
   _____

   "To Build a Fire": _____
   _____
   _____
   _____

2. Describe the **rising action** in each story and the expectations that are generated.
   "The Far and the Near": _____
   _____
   _____
   _____

   "To Build a Fire": _____
   _____
   _____
   _____

3. Does the **rising action** in each story lead to a **climax** or an **anticlimax**? Explain whether the reader's expectations are fulfilled by each.
   _____
   _____
   _____
   _____
   _____
   _____
   _____

"Of Modern Poetry" and **"Anecdote of the Jar"** by Wallace Stevens
"Ars Poetica" by Archibald MacLeish
"Poetry" by Marianne Moore

Literary Analysis: Similes and Metaphors

Similes are a type of figurative language that makes an explicit comparison between two unlike things, connecting them with the word *like* or *as*. **Metaphors** are more direct comparisons. They state not that one thing is *like* something else, but that it *is* that other thing.

Simile: A poem should be wordless/As the flight of birds.
Metaphor: The actor is/A metaphysician in the dark...

DIRECTIONS: Find a simile or a metaphor from each of the following poems. Write it on the line provided. If it is a simile, rewrite it as a metaphor. If it is a metaphor, rewrite it as a simile. Then compare the two forms, explaining why you think the poet chose to use that particular figure of speech. Then answer the questions at the end.

1. Metaphor/Simile from "Of Modern Poetry"

   _____

   _____

   Your rewrite: _____

   Analysis: _____

   _____

2. Metaphor/Simile from "Ars Poetica"

   _____

   _____

   Your rewrite: _____

   Analysis: _____

   _____

3. Metaphor/Simile from "Poetry"

   _____

   _____

   Your rewrite: _____

   Analysis: _____

   _____

4. "Anecdote of the Jar" contains neither metaphors nor similes. What type of figurative language is used? What is the effect of this language?

   _____

   _____

   _____

   _____

Literary Analysis for Enrichment   **45**

Unit 5: Disillusion, Defiance, and Discontent (1914–1946)

"In Another Country" by Ernest Hemingway
"The Corn Planting" by Sherwood Anderson
"A Worn Path" by Eudora Welty

Literary Analysis: A New Point of View

Point of view is the perspective from which a story is told. The most common points of view are first person, omniscient third person, and limited third person. Each point of view has its own impact on the feeling and tone of a story. A story written from the first-person point of view can provide a deeply personal perspective. An advantage of omniscient third-person point of view is that the author can provide insight into the thoughts and feelings of every character.

DIRECTIONS: Identify the point of view in the following passage from "A Worn Path." Then use the space provided to rewrite this passage using a different point of view. Finally, describe how the change in perspective affects the feeling of the passage.

> Pheonix heard the dogs fighting, and heard the man running and throwing sticks. She even heard a gunshot. But she was slowly bending forward by that time, further and further forward, the lids stretched down over her eyes, as if she were doing this in her sleep. Her chin was lowered almost to her knees. The yellow palm of her hand came out from the fold of her apron. Her fingers slid down and along the ground under the piece of money with the grace and care they would have in lifting an egg from under a setting hen.

1. Old point of view: _____

2. New point of view: _____

3. New passage: _____

_____

_____

_____

_____

_____

_____

4. How this new point of view affects the feeling of the passage: _____

_____

_____

_____

Name _____ Date _____

"Chicago" and **"Grass"** by Carl Sandburg

Literary Analysis: Apostrophe and Personification

Apostrophe is the literary technique of directly addressing a person or thing as if that person or thing were present. The speaker of Sandburg's "Chicago" apostrophizes the city. Speaking directly to it implies that it can hear and understand him—so the act of apostrophizing is also an act of **personification.** Speaking to the city lends it human attributes and characteristics.

DIRECTIONS: Find examples of personification in "Chicago" that fit each of the following categories. Then answer the question at the end.

1. Human attributes and feelings: _____

_____

_____

_____

2. Human physical characteristics: _____

_____

_____

_____

3. Human actions: _____

_____

_____

_____

4. What kind of "person" is Chicago? _____

_____

_____

_____

_____

_____

_____

Name _____ Date _____

"The Jilting of Granny Weatherall" by Katherine Anne Porter

Literary Analysis: Comparing Stream of Consciousness

The **stream-of-consciousness** technique in literature mimics real-life thinking processes. A sight, a sound, a flash of memory—any one of these can serve as a trigger, causing a character's thoughts to drift to the past or evoking a personal series of images. Both "Occurrence at Owl Creek Bridge" by Ambrose Bierce and "The Jilting of Granny Weatherall" include passages of stream of consciousness.

DIRECTIONS: Read the following passages. Then answer the questions on the lines provided.

Her eyes opened very wide and the room stood out like a picture she had seen somewhere. Dark colors with the shadows rising towards the ceiling in long angles. The tall black dresser gleamed with nothing on it but John's picture, enlarged from a little one, with John's eyes very black when they should have been blue. You never saw him, so how do you know how he looked? But the man insisted the copy was perfect, it was very rich and handsome. For a picture, yes, but it's not my husband. The table by the bed had a linen cover and a candle and a crucifix. The light was blue from Cornelia's silk lampshades. No sort of light at all, just frippery. You had to live forty years with kerosene lamps to appreciate honest electricity. She felt very strong and she saw Doctor Harry with a rosy nimbus around him.

"You look like a saint, Doctor Harry, and I vow that's as near as you'll ever come to it."

"She's saying something."

—"The Jilting of Granny Weatherall"

As he pushes open the gate and passes up the wide white walk, he sees a flutter of female garments: his wife, looking fresh and cool and sweet, steps down from the veranda to meet him. At the bottom of the steps she stands waiting, with a smile of ineffable joy, an attitude of matchless grace and dignity. Ah, how beautiful she is! He springs forward with extended arms. As he is about to clasp her he feels a stunning blow upon the back of the neck; a blinding white light blazes all about him with a sound like the shock of a cannon—then all is darkness and silence!

—"An Occurrence at Owl Creek Bridge"

1. What is each character thinking about in the stream-of-consciousness section of each passage?

_____

_____

2. What triggers the stream of consciousness in each passage?

_____

_____

3. What ends the stream of consciousness in each passage?

_____

_____

4. How are the two passages similar?

_____

_____

"Race at Morning" and **"Nobel Prize Acceptance Speech"** by William Faulkner

Literary Analysis: Comparing Dialects

Speech that is common to a particular region or group is called **dialect.** Dialect contains variations on standard English, including grammar, pronunciation, and word choice. In the previous unit you read a short story by a master of Midwestern dialect, Mark Twain. Compare Faulkner's use of dialect with Twain's.

DIRECTIONS: Read the passages and answer the questions that follow.

Smiley always come out winner on that pup, till he harnessed a dog once that didn't have no hind legs, because they'd been sawed off in a circular saw, and when the thing had gone along far enough, and the money was all up, and he come to make a snatch for his pet holt, he see in a minute how he'd been imposed on, and how the other dog had him in the door, so to speak...

—"The Notorious Jumping Frog of Calaveras County"

It might 'a' been a signal, a good-bye, a farewell. Still walking, we passed the other three old dogs in the middle of the glade, laying down, too, now jest where they was when the buck vanished, and not trying to get up neither when we passed; and still that hundred yards ahead of them, Eagle, too, not laying down, because he was still on his feet, but his legs was spraddled and his head was down; maybe jest waiting until we was out of sight of his shame, his eyes saying plain as talk when we passed, "I'm sorry boys, but this here is all."

—"Race at Morning"

1. Compare the regional dialects used by Twain and Faulkner. Refer to the stories in your textbook, if necessary. List three similarities.

_____

_____

_____

2. What effect does dialect have on Twain's story?

_____

_____

_____

3. What effect does dialect have on Faulkner's story?

_____

_____

_____

4. These stories are products of different historical eras, yet they are surprisingly similar in style. Explain how the use of dialect contributes to that similarity.

_____

_____

_____

_____

Name _____   Date _____

Literary Analysis: Comparing Blank Verse in Modern Poetry

Blank verse—unrhymed iambic pentameter—has a proud literary history. Shakespeare and other Renaissance dramatists wrote their plays in this meter because it echoes the natural rhythms of spoken English, yet it also can sound formal enough to be appropriate for speeches by the kings, queens, and nobles the actors portrayed.

Robert Frost's poetry is about ordinary, everyday people and things, yet much of it is written in blank verse. What is the effect on the reader?

DIRECTIONS: Reread each of the four poems in this section. Identify whether each poem is or is not blank verse. If it is not blank verse, explain why. Then analyze the overall effect of each poem's rhyme scheme and meter. Compare and contrast structure and meaning, and think about your personal response.

1. "Birches"

   Blank verse?   Yes   No   Why? _____

   Analysis: _____

   _____

   _____

2. "Stopping by Woods on a Snowy Evening"

   Blank verse?   Yes   No   Why? _____

   Analysis: _____

   _____

   _____

3. "Mending Wall"

   Blank verse?   Yes   No   Why? _____

   Analysis: _____

   _____

   _____

4. "Out, Out—"

   Blank verse?   Yes   No   Why? _____

   Analysis: _____

   _____

   _____

5. "Acquainted With the Night"

   Blank verse?   Yes   No   Why? _____

   Analysis: _____

   _____

   _____

"The Night the Ghost Got In" by James Thurber
from *Here Is New York* by E. B. White

Literary Analysis: Informal Essays and Satire

Personal essays are often humorous. One kind of humor often found in a personal essay is **satire**—writing that ridicules or criticizes individuals, ideas, institutions, or social conventions. The tone of satire, which can range from angry to sympathetic, depends on the writer's attitude toward his or her subject. When the police arrive in force in "The Night the Ghost Got In," Thurber's humor takes on a definite satirical edge.

DIRECTIONS: Reread "The Night the Ghost Got In." Answer the questions on the lines provided.

1. At what point did you recognize that Thurber was satirizing the police?

   _____

   _____

   _____

2. What is the effect of the dialogue between various policemen and the narrator and others?

   _____

   _____

   _____

3. Cite an example of dialogue that produces this effect.

   _____

   _____

   _____

4. How would you describe the tone of Thurber's satire?

   _____

   _____

   _____

5. What do you think is Thurber's attitude toward the police? Explain.

   _____

   _____

   _____

6. A *caricature* is a picture of a person or thing in which distinguishing features are ludicrously exaggerated for satirical effect. Is Thurber's portrait of the police a caricature? Explain.

   _____

   _____

   _____

from *Dust Tracks on a Road* by Zora Neale Hurston

Literary Analysis: Comparing Purpose in Autobiography

An **autobiography** is a person's written account of his or her own life, focusing on the events the writer considers most significant. Reasons for writing autobiographies vary widely. Earlier, you read *My Bondage and My Freedom*, the autobiography of Frederick Douglass. How does his purpose in writing compare to Hurston's?

DIRECTIONS: Reread the excerpts from *Dust Tracks on a Road* and *My Bondage and My Freedom*. Answer the questions on the lines provided.

1. What was Douglass's purpose in writing *My Bondage and My Freedom*? What was Hurston's purpose in writing *Dust Tracks on a Road*?

   _____

   _____

   _____

2. What scene or incident from *Dust Tracks on a Road* do you think best serves Hurston's purpose in writing her autobiography? Explain.

   _____

   _____

   _____

3. What scene or incident from *My Bondage and My Freedom* do you think best serves Douglass's purpose in writing his autobiography? Explain.

   _____

   _____

   _____

4. How are Hurston's and Douglass's purposes for writing alike? How are they different?

   _____

   _____

   _____

5. How is this difference reflected in the tone each author uses?

   _____

   _____

   _____

6. Douglass published his autobiography in 1855; Hurston published hers in 1942. To what extent do you think their purposes for writing were shaped by their times? Explain.

   _____

   _____

   _____

"Refugee in America," "Ardella," "The Negro Speaks of Rivers,"
and **"Dream Variations"** by Langston Hughes
"The Tropics in New York" by Claude McKay

Literary Analysis: Comparing Speakers and Using Clues to Identify the Speaker

The **speaker** is the voice of a poem. The speaker may be the poet, another person, an imaginary person, a group of people, an animal, or an object. Often, clues from the poem can help the reader to identify the speaker.

A. DIRECTIONS: Read each of the following passages. Then, on the lines provided, write a sentence or two in which you compare and contrast the speakers in the poems.

> I've known rivers:
> I've known rivers ancient as the world and older than
>   the flow of human blood in human veins.
>
> —"The Negro Speaks of Rivers"

> To fling my arms wide
> In the face of the sun,
> Dance! Whirl! Whirl!
> Till the quick day is done.
>
> —"Dream Variations"

_____

_____

_____

_____

Sometimes a poet deliberately delays revealing the identity of a poem's speaker. Such a delay often helps to build suspense, or a feeling of tension. *Foreshadowing*, or using clues suggestively, can also contribute to a feeling of suspense while ultimately helping the reader to identify the poem's speaker.

B. DIRECTIONS: Reread "The Tropics in New York." Then answer the questions on the lines provided.

1. At what point in "The Tropics in New York" are you sure of the speaker's identity?

_____

_____

2. How does the word *memories* in line 5 help to foreshadow the speaker's identity?

_____

_____

"From the Dark Tower" by Countee Cullen
"A Black Man Talks of Reaping" by Arna Bontemps
"Storm Ending" by Jean Toomer

Literary Analysis: Metaphor and Description

A **metaphor** is an implied comparison between two seemingly dissimilar things. By using a metaphor, a writer can evoke images that may help to communicate his or her message.

Writers often use **description** to develop or heighten their metaphors. Description is writing that captures sights, sounds, smells, tastes, and physical sensations.

DIRECTIONS: Identify the two things being compared in each passage from the poems. Then explain to what senses each description appeals.

1. The night whose sable breast relieves the stark,
   White stars is no less lovely being dark…

   _____

   _____

   _____

2. So in the dark we hid the heart that bleeds,
   And wait, and tend our agonizing seeds.

   _____

   _____

   _____

3. small wonder then my children glean in fields
   They have not sown, and feed on bitter fruit.

   _____

   _____

   _____

4. Thunder blossoms gorgeously above our heads,
   Great, hollow, bell-like flowers,
   Rumbling in the wind…

   _____

   _____

   _____

5. Dripping rain like golden honey—
   And the sweet earth flying from the thunder.

   _____

   _____

   _____

Name _____ Date _____

"The Life You Save May Be Your Own" by Flannery O'Connor

Literary Analysis: Grotesque Characters and Descriptive Details

Some characters in Flannery O'Connor's fiction are **grotesques.** Such characters have a one-track mind; they are controlled by a single emotion, concept, or goal. Passages that describe grotesque characters are often marked by unusual or unexpected **descriptive details.** These details, which appeal to one or more of the five senses, make a vivid impression on the mind of the reader.

DIRECTIONS: Read each passage from the story and locate it in context. Then, on the lines provided, explain how the underlined descriptive details contribute to the portrayal of a grotesque character.

Story Passage	**Details of Grotesque Character Portrayal**
1. He held the pose for almost fifty seconds and then he picked up his box and came on to the porch and dropped down on the bottom step. "Lady," he said in a firm nasal voice, "I'd give a fortune to live where I could see me a sun do that every evening."	_____ _____ _____ _____
2. The daughter was leaning very far down, hanging her head almost between her knees watching him through a triangular door she had made in her overturned hair; and she suddenly fell in a heap on the floor and began to whimper.	_____ _____ _____ _____
3. "What you want her to say next?" Mr. Shiftlet asked. The old woman's smile was broad and toothless and suggestive. "Teach her to say 'sugarpie,' " she said.	_____ _____ _____
4. The boy bent over her and stared at the long pink-gold hair and the half-shut sleeping eyes. Then he looked up and stared at Mr. Shiftlet. "She looks like an angel of Gawd," he murmured.	_____ _____ _____

"The First Seven Years" by Bernard Malamud

Literary Analysis: Epiphany and Round and Dynamic Characters

Characters in literature sometimes have a sudden flash of insight, which is called an **epiphany.** At the moment of an epiphany, the character may realize something significant about himself or herself, about another character, or about life in general. An epiphany is usually but not always associated with a **round character**—one who is complex and multi-faceted—or with a **dynamic character**—one who changes in the course of a work.

DIRECTIONS: Reread each of the following passages in the context of the story. Then, on the lines provided, restate in your own words the epiphany or "moment of insight" that each character experiences. Also tell whether each character is "round" or "dynamic."

Story Passage	Epiphany

1. It broke, the iron striking the floor and jumping with a thump against the wall, but before the enraged shoemaker could cry out, the assistant had torn his hat and coat from the hook and rushed out into the snow.

   _____
   _____
   _____

   Is Sobel a round or a dynamic character? Why?

   _____
   _____

2. When Feld had sufficiently recovered from his anguished disappointment to ask why, she answered without hesitation, "Because he's nothing more than a materialist."

   _____
   _____
   _____

   Do you consider Miriam a round or a dynamic character? Why?

   _____
   _____

3. The room was quiet. Sobel was standing by the window reading, and it was curious that when he read he looked young.
   "She is only nineteen," Feld said brokenly.

   _____
   _____
   _____

   Is Feld a round or a dynamic character, in your opinion? Why?

   _____
   _____
   _____

Name _____ Date _____

"The Brown Chest" by John Updike

Literary Analysis: Atmosphere and Descriptive Detail

Atmosphere is the feeling or mood evoked in the reader by a piece of writing. In fiction, atmosphere arises from events and from descriptions of the setting—especially the effect the setting has on particular characters. To describe the setting, writers use specific details that appeal to one or more of the five senses.

DIRECTIONS: Read each passage in the story. Complete the chart by writing two adjectives that you think best describe the atmosphere or mood created by the passage. Then indicate the specific details in the passage that contribute to this atmosphere.

Story Passage	Atmosphere/Mood
1. Then it moved again. His children, adults all, came from afar and joined him in the house, where their grandmother had at last died, and divided up the furniture—some for them to carry away, some for the local auctioneer to sell, and some for him, the only survivor of that first house, with its long halls and haunted places, to keep and to assimilate to his own house, hundreds of miles away.	_____ _____ Details: _____ _____ _____
2. A little box labelled in his mother's hand-writing "Haircut July 1919" held, wrapped in tissue paper, coils of auburn hair startlingly silky to the touch.	_____ _____ Details: _____ _____ _____
3. On the drive north in a downpour, Gordon had driven the truck, and his father tried to read the map, and in the dim light of the cab failed, and headed him the wrong way out of Westchester County, so they wound up across the Hudson River, amid blinding headlights, on an unfathomable, exitless highway.	_____ _____ Details: _____ _____ _____

"Hawthorne" by Robert Lowell
"Gold Glade" by Robert Penn Warren
"The Light Comes Brighter" by Theodore Roethke
"Traveling Through the Dark" by William Stafford
"The Adamant" by Theodore Roethke

Literary Analysis: Style and Rhyme

Each poet has a unique **style,** or way of putting thoughts into words. A poet's use of rhyme is one key aspect of his or her style. Traditional styles use **exact rhymes,** words that have identical final vowel and consonant sounds. Other styles use **slant rhymes,** words that share ending vowel or consonant sounds but do not rhyme exactly. In the opening stanza of "The Adamant," Roethke uses both types of rhyme:

Thought does not crush to stone.
The great sledge drops in vain.
Truth never is undone;
Its shafts remain.

Stone and *undone* are slant rhymes. *Vain* and *remain* are exact rhymes.

DIRECTIONS: In the columns next to each passage, list the pairs or triplets that are exact rhymes or slant rhymes. Note that you will not fill every box in the chart.

Passage	Exact Rhymes	Slant Rhymes
1. The teeth of knitted gears Turn slowly through the night, But the true substance bears The hammer's weight. —"The Adamant"		
2. The light comes brighter from the east; the caw Of restive crows is sharper on the ear. A walker at the river's edge may hear A cannon crack announce an early thaw. —"The Light Comes Brighter		
3. But high over high rock and leaf-lacing, sky Showed yet bright, and declivity wooed My foot by the quietening stream, and so I Went on, in quiet, through the beech wood: There, in gold light, where the glad gave, it stood. —"Gold Glade"		
4. No, no! in no mansion under earth, Nor imagination's domain of bright air, But solid in soil that gave it its birth, It stands, wherever it is, but somewhere. I shall set my foot, and go there. —"Gold Glade"		

Name _____ Date _____

"Average Waves in Unprotected Waters" by Anne Tyler

Literary Analysis: Comparing Foreshadowing

Many authors use **foreshadowing** to create tension and build suspense. Authors can leave different kinds of details or clues about what will happen later in a plot. They can

- relate events that suggest probable outcomes
- introduce characters that suggest the conflict that will develop
- develop a tone that suggests the story's outcome

For example, Anne Tyler in "Average Waves in Unprotected Waters" and Flannery O'Connor in "The Life You Save May Be Your Own" both use foreshadowing to suggest each story's outcome. Both stories begin with unique or unusual events. The O'Connor story begins when an old woman and her daughter see Mr. Shiflet come "up their road for the first time." In the opening of the Tyler story, Arnold immediately recognizes that "something was up." Both openings foreshadow the life-changing events that will follow.

DIRECTIONS: Fill in the chart with examples of foreshadowing from each story. You can enter exact quotations or summarize the author's use of each foreshadowing technique.

Techniques	Average Waves in Unprotected Waters	The Life You Save May Be Your Own
1. **Events/Situations**		
2. **Characters**		
3. **Tone**		

from *The Names* by N. Scott Momaday
"Mint Snowball" by Naomi Shihab Nye
"Suspended" by Joy Harjo

Literary Analysis: Anecdote and Diction

Authors write **anecdotes,** brief accounts of entertaining or interesting events or experiences, to communicate ideas. The diction they use can help you interpret the author's message or feeling about the anecdote. For example, in one anecdote, N. Scott Momaday says, "My mind loomed upon the farthest edges of the earth, where I could feel the full force of the planet whirling into space." His diction is poetic and elevated. His diction matches the strength and power of his feelings.

DIRECTIONS: The following anecdote from Naomi Shihab Nye's "Mint Snowball" has been rewritten using different diction. On the lines below the two versions, comment on the differences between them.

Nye's version:

My great-grandfather had one specialty: a Mint Snowball which he invented. Some people drove all the way in from Decatur just to taste it. First he stirred fresh mint leaves with sugar and secret ingredients in a small pot on the stove for a very long time. He concocted a flamboyant elixir of mint. Its scent clung to his fingers even after he washed his hands. Then he shaved ice into tiny particles and served it mounted in a glass dish. Permeated with mint syrup. Scoops of rich vanilla ice cream to each side. My mother took a bite of minty ice and ice cream mixed together. The Mint Snowball tasted like winter.

Rewritten version:

My great-grandfather was famous for one weird dessert: a Mint Snowball, which he thought up. Some people drove all the way in from Decatur just to experience it. First he threw fresh mint leaves with sugar and a bunch of other secret stuff in a pot. Then he cooked it forever and a day. He brewed up a wild world of mint. You could smell mint on his fingers even after he washed and washed. Then he chipped ice into tiny bits and served it heaped in a dish. Dripping with mint syrup. Scoops of vanilla ice cream on the side. My mother bit into the minty mess. Eating a Mint Snowball was like munching on a snowman.

_____

_____

_____

_____

_____

_____

_____

Name _____ Date _____

"Everyday Use" by Alice Walker

Literary Analysis: Evaluating Motivations

Analyzing a character's **motivation** can help you to evaluate characters in a story. Thinking about a character's reasons for actions or behaviors allows you to make supported judgments. For example, in "Everyday Use," the character of Dee acts distant when her family's house burns down. Her motivation for this behavior is that she never liked the house and is happy to see it burn. These feelings prevent her from comforting her mother or her sister. Based on these motivations, you might make a judgment that Dee is selfish and uncaring.

DIRECTIONS: Complete this chart to evaluate motivations in "Everyday Use." Describe the character's motivation for each action or behavior. Then evaluate that behavior and make your own judgments.

Action/Behavior	Character's Motivations	My Evaluation
1. Maggie tries to hide when Dee arrives.		
2. Dee changes her name to Wangero.		
3. Dee tries to take quilts made by Grandma Dee.		
4. Maggie says that Dee can have the quilts.		
5. The narrator gives the quilts to Maggie.		

from *The Woman Warrior* by Maxine Hong Kingston

Literary Analysis: Comparing Memoirs

Authors write **memoirs** to share personal experiences and insights with readers. An author's method of writing a memoir gives a reader clues about the author's feelings and perspectives. For example, both N. Scott Momaday's *The Names* and Maxine Hong Kingston's *The Woman Warrior* are memoirs. In the selections you have read, Momaday describes important events in his own childhood, events that helped to shape his personality and beliefs. Kingston focuses on one important day in her mother's life. Her mother's actions and reactions reflect many vital parts of her personality.

DIRECTIONS: Answer these questions to compare the selections you have read from *The Names* and from *The Woman Warrior.*

1. From what narrative point of view is *The Names* told?

   _____

2. From what narrative point of view is *The Woman Warrior* told?

   _____

3. Why do you think Momaday and Kingston chose different narrative points of view?

   _____

   _____

4. Which event described in *The Names* do you think is most important to the narrator? Why?

   _____

   _____

5. Which event described in *The Woman Warrior* do you think is most important to the main character? Why?

   _____

6. Describe one insight that a reader might gain by reading the personal experiences recounted in *The Names.*

   _____

   _____

7. Describe one insight that a reader might gain by reading the personal experiences recounted in *The Woman Warrior.*

   _____

   _____

8. Imagine that you could meet a character described in one of these memoirs. Which character would you like to meet? Why?

   _____

   _____

"Antojos" by Julia Alvarez

Literary Analysis: How Flashbacks Help Reveal Character and Theme

A **flashback** is a scene or event from an earlier time that interrupts the chronological order of a story. Writers use flashbacks to provide important details about the backgrounds, personalities, and motives of **characters**. Flashbacks can also help reveal a work's **theme.** Early in "Antojos," a flashback gives readers a glimpse of a conversation between Yolanda and her aunts in the capital.

DIRECTIONS: Reread the flashback that begins with the paragraph starting, "In the capital, her aunts had plied her..." On the lines below, identify the specific passages in the flashback that furnish the reader with important background information. Then explain what the quoted passage reveals about the character or the theme.

1. Why do the aunts want to spoil Yolanda?

   Exact words from the text:

   _____

   _____

   What the quotation reveals:

   _____

2. What is the meaning of the story's title?

   Exact words from the text:

   _____

   _____

   What the quotation reveals:

   _____

3. How do you learn that Yolanda's Spanish is no longer fluent?

   Exact words from the text:

   _____

   _____

   What the quotation reveals:

   _____

4. Where does the writer refer to the mysterious beliefs of people in the countryside?

   Exact words from the text:

   _____

   _____

   What the quotation reveals:

   _____

   _____

"Freeway 280" by Lorna Dee Cervantes
"Who Burns for the Perfection of Paper" by Martín Espada
"Hunger in New York City" by Simon Ortiz
"Most Satisfied by Snow" by Diana Chang
"What For" by Garrett Hongo

Literary Analysis: Comparing Voices

Just as every person has his or her own way of speaking, every poet has an individual **voice.** A poet's distinctive sound is based on word choice and combinations, rhyme (or lack of it), pace, attitude, and even the pattern of vowels and consonants.

DIRECTIONS: Read the following passages. Use the Venn diagram to compare the voices in the passages. Remember that you can base your comparisons on what you hear, including word choice, rhyme, pace, and attitude. Place shared elements in the overlapping region. Place elements unique to each passage in that passage's separate region.

1. Maybe it's here
   en los campos extraños de esta ciudad
   where I'll find it, that part of me
   mown under
   like a corpse
   or a loose seed.

   —"Freeway 280"

2. Ten years later, in law school,
   I knew that every legal pad
   was glued with the sting of hidden cuts,
   that every open lawbook
   was a pair of hands
   upturned and burning.

   —"Who Burns for the Perfection of Paper"

3. I wanted to become a doctor of pure magic,
   to string a necklace of sweet words
   fragrant as pine needles and plumeria,
   fragrant as the bread my mother baked,
   place it like a lei of cowrie shells
   and *pikake* flowers around my father's neck…

   —"What For"

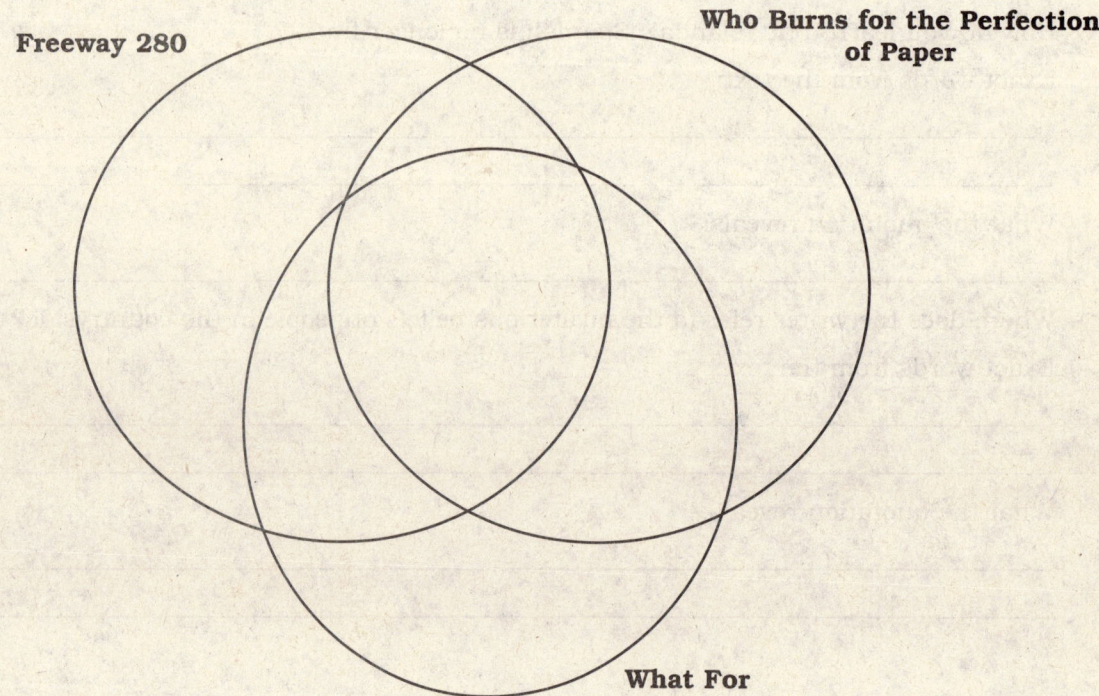

from *The Mortgaged Heart* by Carson McCullers
"Onomatopoeia" by William Safire
"Coyote v. Acme" by Ian Frazier

Literary Analysis: Essays and Tone

The **tone** of a literary work is the writer's attitude toward his or her subject, characters, or audience. A writer's tone may be formal or informal, friendly or distant, personal or pompous. Authors of essays choose a specific tone to help them achieve the goal of their writing. For example, Carson McCullers's tone in *The Mortgaged Heart* is serious, personal, and reflective. This tone is effective for her analytic essay because it engages the reader's attention and demonstrates the author's careful consideration of the topic.

DIRECTIONS: First, classify each essay as analytic, expository, or satiric. Next, supply two quotations that you feel accurately reflect the tone of the entire essay. Finally, describe the tone of each essay using your own words.

Essay	Kind of Essay	Two Examples of Tone	Tone
1. *The Mortgaged Heart* by Carson McCullers			
2. "Onomatopoeia" by William Safire			
3. "Coyote v. Acme" by Ian Frazier			

"Straw Into Gold" by Sandra Cisneros
"For the Love of Books" by Rita Dove
"Mother Tongue" by Amy Tan

Literary Analysis: Tone in a Reflective Essay

A writer's attitude toward his or her subject, characters, or audience is evident in the tone of a work. When you are reading an essay, you need to pay as much attention to the writer's tone as you would when you are listening to someone's voice.

DIRECTIONS: Read each of the following passages. What attitude do you hear in the author's voice? Identify that attitude or tone on the lines below each passage. Finally, based on these three essays, draw a conclusion about tone in a reflective essay.

"Straw Into Gold" by Sandra Cisneros

1. Thinking back and looking at that photograph documenting the three of us consuming those lopsided circles I am amazed. Just as I am amazed I could finish my MFA exam (lopsided and crooked, but finished all the same). Didn't think I could do it. But I did.

   Tone: _____

   _____

2. I like to think my parents were preparing me all along for my life as an artist even though they didn't know it. From my father I inherited a love of wandering. He was born in Mexico City but as a young man he traveled into the U.S. vagabonding.

   Tone: _____

   _____

"For the Love of Books" by Rita Dove

3. Then there was Shakespeare—daunting for many years because it was his entire oeuvre, in matching wine-red volumes that were so thick that they looked more like over-sized bouillon cubes than books, and yet it was that ponderous title—*The Complete Works of William Shakespeare*—that enticed me, because here was a lifetime's work—a lifetime!—in two compact, dense packages.

   Tone: _____

   _____

"Mother Tongue" by Amy Tan

4. Lately, I've been giving more thought to the kind of English my mother speaks. Like others, I have described it to people as "broken," or "fractured" English. But I wince when I say that. It has always bothered me that I can think of no way to describe it other than "broken," as if it were damaged and needed to be fixed, as if it lacked a certain wholeness and soundness.

   Tone: _____

   _____

5. Conclusions about tone: _____

   _____

   _____

Name _____ Date _____

"The Rockpile" by James Baldwin

Literary Analysis: Setting, Character, and Symbol

The setting of a story often has a direct impact on the characters in the story. For example, a setting may limit a character's choices or expand them; a setting may prove helpful, have a calming influence, or be the source of some other benefit. A setting can also be symbolic; that is, it can serve in the story as the place or thing itself but also have other meanings.

DIRECTIONS: Answer the questions to explore how the setting in "The Rockpile" affects the characters and to explain what the rockpile symbolizes.

1. The family in this story lives in an apartment building in Harlem. What options for play do the children have on the apparently nice day on which the story takes place?

   _____

   _____

   _____

2. What personality traits displayed by Roy and John might be the product of the setting in which they live?

   _____

   _____

3. The adults in this story brand some parts of this setting as "sinful." What places do they consider "sinful"?

   _____

   _____

4. Why is the rockpile forbidden to the children?

   _____

   _____

5. What makes the rockpile so attractive to the children?

   _____

   _____

   _____

6. What does the rockpile symbolize? Include a discussion of its physical features. Why do you think Baldwin chose it as his title?

   _____

   _____

   _____

   _____

   _____

   _____

from _Hiroshima_ by John Hersey
"Losses" and "The Death of the Ball Turret Gunner" by Randall Jarrell

Literary Analysis: Comparing Implied Themes

An **implied theme** is a central message about life that is not stated directly in a selection. You can discover an implied theme by closely studying the writer's choice of details, portrayal of characters and events, and use of literary devices. Often, you can discover the same implied theme in two or more selections. Each writer may use different details and devices in order to imply the same theme.

DIRECTIONS: For each theme, give a specific example from each selection cited to show how that theme is implied.

1. **Implied theme:** War is a dehumanizing experience.

   Hiroshima: _____
   _____
   _____

   "Losses": _____
   _____
   _____

   "The Death of the Ball Turret Gunner":_____
   _____
   _____

2. **Implied theme:** War seems to choose its victims arbitrarily.

   Hiroshima: _____
   _____
   _____

   "Losses": _____
   _____
   _____

3. **Implied theme:** War results in seemingly senseless loss.

   Hiroshima: _____
   _____
   _____

   "Losses": _____
   _____
   _____

"Mirror" by Sylvia Plath
"In a Classroom" by Adrienne Rich
"The Explorer" by Gwendolyn Brooks
"Frederick Douglass" and **"Runagate Runagate"** by Robert Hayden

Literary Analysis: Comparing and Contrasting Themes and Contexts

The historical or biographical **context** of a poem can help you understand its central message, or **theme.** Context can be very important in a poem. In some cases, if a particular poem were written in a different context, the poem would be unable to express the same theme.

DIRECTIONS: Answer the following questions, based on what you know about the biographical and historical context of the poems you have read.

1. Considering what you know about the life of Sylvia Plath, why is it unlikely that she would have ever written the poem "Runagate Runagate"? How does the theme of "Runagate Runagate" run contrary to Plath's personality and behavior?

   _____

   _____

   _____

   _____

2. Imagine that "Mirror" had been written by Gwendolyn Brooks. Given what you know about the biographical context of Brooks's life, how would the theme of "Mirror" be different?

   _____

   _____

   _____

   _____

3. How are the themes of "In a Classroom" and "Runagate Runagate" different from each other? What is different about the historical context in which each poem was written?

   _____

   _____

   _____

   _____

4. Considering the biographical contexts of the two authors, why is it less likely that Sylvia Plath would have written "Frederick Douglass" than, say, Gwendolyn Brooks?

   _____

   _____

   _____

   _____

"For My Children" by Colleen McElroy
"Bidwell Ghost" by Louise Erdrich

Literary Analysis: Comparing and Contrasting Lyric Poetry

Lyric poetry is brief and melodic. It focuses on a single experience or subject, expresses the speaker's observations and feelings about the subject, and creates an overall effect. Although all lyric poems have elements in common, you can also find differences among them.

DIRECTIONS: Answer the following questions to compare and contrast the two lyric poems "For My Children" and "Bidwell Ghost."

1. How is the single experience or subject of "For My Children" similar to and different from the single experience or subject of "Bidwell Ghost"?

   Similar: _____

   _____

   _____

   Different: _____

   _____

   _____

2. How are the speaker's observations and feelings about the subject of "For My Children" similar to and different from the speaker's observations and feelings about the subject of "Bidwell Ghost"?

   Similar: _____

   _____

   _____

   Different: _____

   _____

   _____

3. How is the overall effect of "For My Children" similar to and different from the overall effect of "Bidwell Ghost"?

   Similar: _____

   _____

   _____

   Different: _____

   _____

   _____

"The Writer in the Family" by E. L. Doctorow

Literary Analysis: Static and Dynamic Characters in Conflict

You can analyze story characters by the way they think, speak, and behave. A **static character** does not change much in thinking, speech, or actions throughout a story. A **dynamic character,** by contrast, does change significantly in thinking, speech, or actions by the end of the story.

Characters in a story are usually in some type of **conflict**—a struggle between opposing forces. A conflict between two or more characters is an external conflict. A conflict within a character is an internal conflict.

DIRECTIONS: Answer the following questions to analyze the characters in conflict in "The Writer in the Family."

1. a. The central conflict is between Jonathan and which other character?

   _____

   b. How is this conflict resolved?

   _____

   c. How does this resolution help show who is a dynamic and who is a static character?

   _____

2. a. Jonathan is also experiencing an internal conflict. What is it about?

   _____

   _____

   b. How is this conflict resolved?

   _____

   _____

   c. How does this resolution help show whether Jonathan is a dynamic or a static character?

   _____

3. a. With whom is Jonathan's mother in conflict?

   _____

   b. Is the conflict resolved? Explain.

   _____

   _____

   c. How does this help show whether Jonathan's mother is a dynamic or a static character?

   _____

"**Camouflaging the Chimera**" by Yusef Komunyakaa
"**Ambush**" by Tim O'Brien

Literary Analysis: The Narrator in Nonfiction

A narrative may have a **first-person narrator** or a **third-person narrator.** A first-person narrator often reveals his or her inner thoughts. First-person narration usually enables you to discover the narrator's personality, viewpoints, and personal responses. In *fiction,* a third-person narrator may know and relate the inner thoughts of one or more characters. In *nonfiction,* however, third-person narration does not always allow you to get inside a character's head in the same way. The story may leave you with a different kind of information and a different impression if narrated in third person instead of first person.

Both "Camouflaging the Chimera" and "Ambush" are based on nonfictional experiences and written in the first person.

> It was entirely automatic. I did not hate the young man; I did not see him as the enemy;
> I did not ponder issues of morality or politics or military duty.

This passage from "Ambush," for example, allows the reader to know that issues of hatred, morality, politics, and duty have nothing to do with the narrator's actions. With third-person narration, a reader might logically assume he lobbed the grenade for one of those reasons.

DIRECTIONS: For the following lines, explain how your understanding might be altered if the story were narrated in third person instead of first person.

"Camouflaging the Chimera"

1. We wove/ourselves into the terrain,/content to be a hummingbird's target.

   _____

   _____

   _____

2. The river ran/through our bones.

   _____

   _____

3. …a world revolved/under each man's eyelid.

   _____

   _____

"Ambush"

4. It was a difficult moment, but I did what seemed right, which was to say, "Of course not," and then to take her onto my lap and hold her for a while.

   _____

   _____

   _____

5. He was a short, slender young man of about twenty. I was afraid of him—afraid of something—and as he passed me on the trail I threw a grenade that exploded at his feet and killed him.

   _____

   _____

Name _____ Date _____

The Crucible, **Act I,** by Arthur Miller

Literary Analysis: Characterization Through Dialogue and Stage Directions

Dialogue is the words that characters in drama speak. **Stage directions,** among other information, tell how characters in a drama behave—what actions they take, what tone of voice they use, what their motivations might be.

Characterization is the way a writer reveals a character's personality. A playwright reveals characters through the dialogue and the stage directions.

DIRECTIONS: Read the following dialogue and stage directions. Then answer the questions about what each character's words and actions reveal.

> **PARRIS:** I cannot blink what I saw, Abigail, for my enemies will not blink it. I saw a dress lying on the grass.
>
> **ABIGAIL,** *innocently:* A dress?
>
> **PARRIS,** *it is very hard to say:* Aye, a dress. And I thought I saw—someone naked running through the trees.
>
> **ABIGAIL,** *in terror:* No one was naked! You mistake yourself, uncle!
>
> **PARRIS,** *with anger:* I saw it! *He moves from her. Then, resolved:* Now tell me true, Abigail. And I pray you feel the weight of truth upon you, for now my ministry's at stake, my ministry and perhaps your cousin's life. Whatever abomination you have done, give me all of it now, for I dare not to be taken unaware when I go before them down there.

1. What kind of a person is Abigail? Cite two examples from the dialogue or stage directions to explain your answer.

   _____

   _____

   _____

2. Why do you think Parris finds it "very hard to say" that he saw someone naked?

   _____

   _____

3. Why does Abigail respond "in terror"?

   _____

   _____

4. Why do you think the playwright specifies that Parris "moves from her"?

   _____

   _____

5. Based on this passage, what is Parris most concerned with? Cite at least one piece of dialogue to support your answer.

   _____

   _____

   _____

Name _____ Date _____

The Crucible, **Act II,** by Arthur Miller

Literary Analysis: Comparing the Use of Allusion

An **allusion** is a reference to a well-known person, place, event, literary work, or work of art. Writers often make allusions to stories from the Bible, to Greek and Roman myths, to Shakespearean plays, and to political and historical events. With an allusion, a writer can bring to mind a complex idea clearly and simply.

DIRECTIONS: Answer these questions to compare and contrast two writers' use of the element of allusion.

1. What poem that you read in Unit 6, Part 3, has an allusion in its title?

   _____

2. What type of allusion is it?

   _____

3. Explain the meaning of the allusion.

   _____

   _____

   _____

   _____

4. Would a biblical or Roman or Shakespearean allusion also have been appropriate for the poet to use? Explain your answer.

   _____

   _____

   _____

   _____

5. What type of allusion is found in *The Crucible*?

   _____

6. Why do you think Miller used this type of allusion for the characters in *The Crucible* to speak?

   _____

7. Would Greek or Roman or Shakespearean allusions been appropriate in *The Crucible*? Explain your answer.

   _____

   _____

   _____

   _____

Name _____ Date _____

The Crucible, **Act III**, by Arthur Miller

Literary Analysis: Dramatic Irony in Plot

Irony occurs when appearances differ from reality, or when what you expect differs from what actually happens. **Dramatic irony** occurs when characters believe one thing while the audience knows that something else is true.

Much of the plot of *The Crucible* involves dramatic irony. The **plot** is the sequence of events in the drama. In a plot, an inciting incident introduces the central conflict. The conflict then increases during the development of the plot until it reaches a high point of interest or tension—the climax.

DIRECTIONS: Answer the questions to determine how dramatic irony plays a key role in the plot of *The Crucible*.

1. What does the audience know about the girls that many of the characters—including Danforth—originally do not know?

   _____

   _____

   _____

2. What does the audience know about Abigail that many of the characters—including Danforth—originally do not know?

   _____

   _____

   _____

3. There are many conflicts in *The Crucible*. What is the central conflict involving John Proctor?

   _____

   _____

   _____

4. What is the climax of *The Crucible*—the scene where the conflict reaches the greatest dramatic tension? Explain your answer.

   _____

   _____

   _____

   _____

5. Why is this climax an example of dramatic irony?

   _____

   _____

   _____

   _____

The Crucible, **Act IV,** by Arthur Miller

Literary Analysis: Characters and Theme

An **theme** is a central idea or insight that a writer tries to convey in a literary work. A work of literature may have more than one theme. Themes of The Crucible include the following:

- political paranoia
- justice/injustice
- fear
- guilt
- revenge

- pride
- intolerance
- authority
- integrity
- courage

In a play, **characters** are revealed by what they do, whay they say, and what other characters say about them. Often, a playwright will choose one or more characters to carry a theme. The characters' behavior will help crystallize the theme, showing, for example, what *integrity*, *revenge,* or *intolerance* might look like and what its consequences might be.

DIRECTIONS: Write a few sentences telling how each character represents one or more themes of *The Crucible.* Give specific examples of things that the character does and says, and things that are said about that character, to show how the playwright has used that character to explore one or more themes.

Rebecca Nurse

_____

_____

_____

_____

Deputy Governor Danforth

_____

_____

_____

_____

Mary Warren

_____

_____

_____

_____

John Proctor

_____

_____

_____

_____

Another character of your choice

_____

_____

_____